Hiking
with
Jesus

Also by James Feldbush:
Eye-openers

To order, call 1-800-765-6955.

Visit us at www.reviewandherald.com for information on other Review and Herald® products.

Hiking
With
Jesus

Jim Feldbush

REVIEW AND HERALD® PUBLISHING ASSOCIATION
Since 1861 | www.reviewandherald.com

The author assumes full responsibility for the accuracy of all facts and quotations as cited in this book.

All Bible texts are from the *Holy Bible, New International Version.* Copyright © 1973, 1978, 1984, International Bible Society. Used by permission of Zondervan Bible Publishers.

This book was
Edited by Andy Nash
Copyedited by Delma Miller and James Cavil
Designed by Tina M. Ivany
Cover and interior art by Dan Sharp
Electronic makeup by Shirley M. Bolivar
Typeset: Futura 12.5/16

PRINTED IN U.S.A.

12 11 10   5 4 3

R&H Cataloging Service
Feldbush, James, 1958-
     Hiking with Jesus.

     1. Children—Religious life.   2. Devotional literature—Juvenile.
3. Devotional calendars—Seventh-day Adventist.   I. Title.

                              242.62

ISBN 978-0-8280-1584-4

This book is dedicated to

Mom and Dad,
who instilled in me a love for nature and the Bible.

Thanks!

Dear Caring Adult,

Thank you for taking time to read with your young person—reading has great educational benefits. Reading from and about God's Word has incomparable eternal benefits.

This book was written with several principles in mind:

•*Hiking With Jesus* explores the world of nature. Almost every page of the Bible contains a story or illustration from the natural world. That's why nature is often referred to as God's second book. There are so many lessons to learn from birds, trees, and rocks. That's what we'll be exploring this year.

•This book will take you and your child through the entire Bible. The first reading begins in the first chapter of Genesis, and the last reading ends in the last chapter of Revelation. The readings in between are based on Scripture from every book in the Bible. Not many devotional books do that!

•Although its daily readings are from God's Word, this book is not meant to take the place of the Bible. Please use this book as an opening into a deeper study of the Scriptures. Explore other verses in the same Bible book you're reading from on a particular day. Use a concordance and hunt down instances in other parts of the Bible of the same tree or flower you are studying. God will speak to you and your child in this way.

•Concepts will be repeated. Repetition is a proven educational technique. It helps adults, as well as children, remember the things they've studied. You will see a number of concepts repeated throughout the book. This happened naturally as I discovered them in God's Word. If God thought some things were worth repeating, He must have decided they were pretty important.

•Refer to God's second book in everyday life. During the day, as you see trees, rocks, and birds, point them out to your child and remember the lessons God taught you from His Word. That's exactly why He used these objects of nature!

•Most important, ask for God's Holy Spirit to teach you and your child each day. The Holy Spirit is the "inspirer" of God's Word. He's the best one to instruct us in its meaning for our lives. Ask for His presence as you study each day.

Now, let's get ready for an exciting year as we dig into God's Word and learn from the world of nature. This will be fun!

Sincerely,

Jim Feldbush

Hi, Boys and Girls!

I'm so excited that you've joined me on this adventure. And it really is an adventure! Did you know that hidden in every book of the Bible—almost on every page of the Bible—is a bug or a bird or a rock or something from God's wonderful world of nature?

If you'll look closely, God talks about nature again and again in His Word. There's something very special about the things He's created. That's exactly why we're going to spend this year together digging up as many insects and collecting as many rocks and looking at as many animals as we can find in the pages of God's Word. Each day we'll look at something God wanted us to know about nature. We'll start with the book of Genesis and explore every book of the Bible until we get to Revelation. By the time we're done, we'll have hiked through the entire Bible! You'll be a real Bible-nature-scholar-adventurer!

So get out your magnifying glass, rock pick, butterfly net, and binoculars. God has so much nature He wants to share with you. The best part of all is this: Whenever you see a bird or a rock or a tree or a flower, you'll remember the important nature lessons God has taught us from His Word.

Put on your boots! Get out your Bible! Let's hit the trail!

—Jim Feldbush

Just Reflecting

God made two great lights—the greater light to govern the day and the lesser light to govern the night. Genesis 1:16.

The greater light and the lesser light—what do you think those are? If you said the greater light is the sun and the lesser light is the moon, you're right! Today, during our first hike of the year, we'll be looking to the skies to help us understand more about God's love.

The sun is called the greater light because it's brighter, and the moon is called the lesser light because it's not as bright. Do you know why the moon isn't as bright? Because the moon is just reflecting the light of the sun. It doesn't even make its own light!

Did you know that you and I can be like the moon? We can reflect God's love and light. God's light is so bright that if you choose to talk with Him each day and read the Bible, pretty soon people will see Jesus' love reflecting off you. Now, that's truly amazing. Let's look to the true "Son" of the universe today and let Him bounce His love off us and onto others.

Breathe Deep!

The Lord God formed the man from the dust of the ground and breathed into his nostrils the breath of life, and the man became a living being. Genesis 2:7.

Stop! Think! What are you doing right now that you don't even have to think about? Go ahead—say it out loud. Did you say breathing? You are right! Breathing is called an involuntary action. That means your brain tells your lungs to breathe without you thinking about it.

It works this way. When you breathe in through your nose or mouth the air goes down a tube called the trachea and into your lungs. When the air is in your lungs, tiny blood vessels on the inside of your lungs take the oxygen and carry it to all the parts of your body that need it. Your muscles need it to work, your brain needs it to work, even your heart needs it to work.

We might not always realize it, but you and I need Jesus even more than air. Without Him, you and I cannot live eternally with Him. Breathe in lots of Jesus today by reading His Word and talking with Him in prayer. As we hike through the Bible together this year, don't forget—breathe deep!

It's a Colorful World

*The gold of that land is good; aromatic resin
and onyx are also there. Genesis 2:12.*

For today's hike you'll need a hammer, a chisel, and a rock collector's bag to sling over your shoulder. We're going rock collecting! The rock we're looking for today is called onyx.

What does onyx look like? Well, the next time you walk past a candy store, just turn around and walk right in. Ask for the licorice. No, not the long stringy kind, but the kind that comes in little squares and has several layers of many colors. That's what onyx looks like. It's a very pretty, many-colored stone that people have used for thousands of years to decorate with.

All those layers of different colors in the onyx stone are like all the different people of the world. We're all different. Some have different ideas, some have different hair, some have different talents, and some have different skin. Together we make a beautiful picture of God's world. Rather than being bothered by the differences in the people around us, let's enjoy those differences just as God enjoys them.

Can You Take a Ribbin'?

The Lord God caused the man to fall into a deep sleep; and while he was sleeping, he took one of the man's ribs and closed up the place with flesh. Genesis 2:21.

Watch out! Today we're taking a hike through the Garden of Eden. You don't want to step on Adam and Eve. Shhh. They're sleeping. Watch as God removes a rib from Adam and uses it to create Eve. What an amazing God He is!

Can you feel your ribs? Do you know what they do? They protect your internal organs. If you didn't have ribs, your heart, lungs, and other important organs would be damaged almost every time you fell. Your ribs are made of bone, but they're connected to your breastbone with cartilage. Your breastbone is that bone going up and down in the middle of your chest. The cartilage makes your rib cage flexible so it doesn't break each time you fall on your back or chest or side. It's true, your ribs are very important protectors.

You and I have God's protectors around us, too! They're His angels. He sends them to watch over and protect us each and every day. I'm so glad the angels are looking out for us. Doesn't it feel good to be loved and protected?

Run! It's a Flood!

Noah was six hundred years old when the floodwaters came on the earth. Genesis 7:6.

Quick, get on your raincoat and boots and run for the ark! There's no time to lose. I imagine it would have been a very fast hike if I had believed Noah and had decided to run to the safety of the ark.

Floodwaters can be very dangerous. A violent storm can cause so much water to rush to a spot that people and animals have to climb to the tops of their houses or to the nearest mountain. Some people have lost their homes, and some have even lost their lives. They were saved only if there was a place or a person to run to.

It was like that with Noah's flood, only worse. Many people lost their eternal lives that day. Only those who ran to the safety of the ark were saved. It will be like that one day when Jesus comes again. Only those who have run to Jesus and know Him will be saved. I'm glad we're hiking through the Bible together. It means that every day we're getting to know Jesus and are safe in His arms—the only arms that can save us for eternity.

Spring Up, O Well

Now the springs of the deep and the floodgates of the heavens had been closed, and the rain had stopped falling from the sky. Genesis 8:2.

The springs of the deep and the floodgates of the heavens had been closed—and was Noah glad! He'd been in the ark a long time and was ready to get on some dry land. Where had all that water come from? Well, some came from above—rain; and some came from below—springs. Did you know that there is water under the earth?

Have you ever thought about where water goes when it rains? There aren't very many places it can go. Much of it soaks into the ground and sinks into little tunnels and caves underground. But all that water doesn't stay underground forever. It comes up again in different places all around the world. Sometimes it bubbles up slowly and makes an above-ground river. Sometimes it comes out of the ground with such force that it shoots many feet into the air. Then it's called a geyser.

When it was time for the Flood to end, God just closed up the earth so the springs wouldn't flow anymore. God is so powerful; imagine what He can do for you. Why don't you ask Him today to help you be a spring of His love?

It's a Long Climb

The waters continued to recede until the tenth month, and on the first day of the tenth month the tops of the mountains became visible. Genesis 8:5.

Have you ever hiked to the top of a mountain? Maybe you've been to Colorado and hiked to the top of a mountain more than 14,000 feet above sea level. Some have even climbed to the top of the world's highest mountain, Mount Everest. Mount Everest is more than five miles high. It's so high that most people who climb it must wear oxygen tanks because the air is so thin. It's a very dangerous mountain to climb because it's covered with so much snow and ice. Furious storms can blow in at any time.

We talked about Noah's flood yesterday. Today we want to talk about when the rain ended. The water started to go down after many months, and finally Noah could see the tops of mountains. Finally there was hope. Land had appeared!

Sometimes there are problems in life like that. We can't see any hope. But just wait—God will always give you some hope. He might be teaching you a very important lesson. Wait on Him, and finally you'll see the tops of your mountains. He'll give you hope again. Continue to trust in Him!

The Bright Side of Life

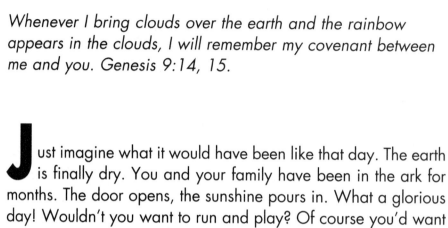

Whenever I bring clouds over the earth and the rainbow appears in the clouds, I will remember my covenant between me and you. Genesis 9:14, 15.

Just imagine what it would have been like that day. The earth is finally dry. You and your family have been in the ark for months. The door opens, the sunshine pours in. What a glorious day! Wouldn't you want to run and play? Of course you'd want to take a hike and look around to see what you can find.

But wait. God says you need to do something special first. Noah builds an altar to God to thank Him for keeping his family safe. What's that? It's made up of many colors. It's huge. It's a rainbow! It's God's promise that an earth-destroying flood will never happen again, and when God makes a promise, He keeps it.

The Bible is full of God's promises. If you start reading and looking for them you'll find many of them. Read Psalm 34:7. You'll find a wonderful promise that says God will always protect you. And there are hundreds more. I'm so glad God sends His rainbow of promises in the Bible. It helps me know He loves us and wants the very best for our lives.

I'm Hungry

Now there was a famine in the land, and Abram went down to Egypt to live there for a while because the famine was severe. Genesis 12:10.

As we hike right into Genesis 12:10 we find Abram hiking to Egypt. He was hiking there because there was a famine in his homeland. A famine happens when there's not enough food to feed all the people in the land. It usually happens because there's been no rain and the crops won't grow. This famine was so bad that Abram went to another country to live for a while.

Have you ever been that hungry—so hungry that you had to move to another country to find food? Most of us have never experienced that. People who experience famines are desperate for food. They'll do almost anything to get food.

Leaving God out of your life can cause a famine too. Not a famine of food, but a famine of God's guidance. We need Him so much each day to help us make the right decisions for our lives. Only He knows the beginning from the end and can help us hike down the path that leads to eternal life. Don't have a "God famine." He's right here, right now. Talk to Him and let Him feed you with wisdom.

10
JANUARY

Don't Fall In

Now the Valley of Siddim was full of tar pits, and when the kings of Sodom and Gomorrah fled, some of the men fell into them and the rest fled to the hills. Genesis 14:10.

Careful now. Slowly walk to the edge and look in. See that black ooze bubbling up to the top? That's tar. Do you know where we've hiked to today? It's the La Brea Tar Pits in Los Angeles, California. But we didn't come just to see the stuff they put on roads for cars to drive on. Let's go into the George C. Page Museum.

Look at all those bones! There's thousands of them. Actually, since 1906 more than 1 million bones have been taken from the tar pits. The bones haven't decayed because there's very little oxygen trapped in the tar. I guess that would mean the kings that fell into the tar pits in our verse today might still be there! Yuck!

God can preserve something for you too. The Bible says that God will preserve us in "perfect peace" if we trust in Him. You can read all about it in Isaiah 26:3. We sure wouldn't want to fall into the tar pits, but we can be safe falling into God's arms. He's promised to keep us in "perfect peace."

No Yoke for Me!

The Lord said to him, "Bring me a heifer, a goat and a ram, each three years old, along with a dove and a young pigeon." Genesis 15:9.

Today we hike to the farm. We're looking for a heifer, just like the one God asked Abram to bring Him in the verse above. A heifer is a young cow that hasn't had any babies yet. God asked Abram to bring a heifer because God wanted to make a promise to Abram.

Sometimes the Israelites brought captives back from war or goods they had captured. Sometimes an Israelite had become unclean in some way. When these things happened God asked His people to sacrifice a red heifer. Just as He asked of Abram, one of the special requirements was that this red cow must never have had a yoke on its neck before. A yoke is what the Israelites would put on the cow's neck so it could pull a plow or wagon.

God doesn't want you to have Satan's yoke around your neck either. He doesn't want you to mess around with sin, get yourself in trouble, and suffer the guilt and consequences that sin brings. God wants you to live a guilt-free life of peace. Trust and obey Him today and see how good it feels to be free of Satan's yoke.

You're Not Too Young?

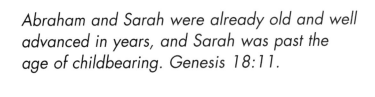

Abraham and Sarah were already old and well advanced in years, and Sarah was past the age of childbearing. Genesis 18:11.

Today we're hiking to the hospital's nursery. We're going to see the babies. Quiet now. Aren't they cute? God made us in such a wonderful way. I'm glad moms and dads can have babies and form families.

Our verse for today says that Sarah was past the age of childbearing. When moms get older they can't have babies anymore. Sarah was at that age. She was nearly 100 years old! She actually laughed at the idea. But do you know what happened? That's right, God performed a miracle and Sarah had a baby when no one, including her, thought it was possible.

Sometimes people might think that you're too young to do anything important for God. Do you believe that? I hope not! You are never too young to put a smile on your face and brighten someone's day. You're never too young to help someone with a job they have to do, and you're never too young to tell someone about Jesus. It's true—just like God helped Sarah have a baby when she thought she was too *old*, God can help you to bring others to Him no matter how *young* you are.

Getting over the Hump

When the camels had finished drinking, the man took out a gold nose ring weighing a beka and two gold bracelets weighing ten shekels. Genesis 24:22.

Camels, camels, camels—you find them everywhere in the Bible. Maybe you and I can take a rest from our hike today and just ride a camel! Camels were like cars for Bible people. They hauled the groceries, took their riders to church and even on a Sunday afternoon drive if they just wanted to see the sights.

I think the most amazing thing about the useful camel is that it can go for months without water. Camels drink gallons at a time when they're thirsty. The water they drink is stored in the fatty hump on their back. You can always tell when a camel needs more water, because its hump starts to sag.

God made the very cool camel in such a wonderful way. They were and still are very useful animals. God can make you useful for Him, also. He has given you special talents and gifts so you can tell other people about Him in your own unique way. But you must make the choice to be useful for God. Let's ask Him today to use us to tell others about His love.

14 JANUARY

Way Down Deep

That day Isaac's servants came and told him about the well they had dug. They said, "We've found water!" Genesis 26:32.

Make sure you have your hiking boots on today. When those well diggers hit water it's liable to shoot right up the drill hole and get you wet. Our verse for today shows us that people have been digging for water for thousands of years. We need it to drink, bathe, and take care of our animals.

Sometimes well diggers have to drill hundreds of feet down into the earth to find water. On January 6 we talked about underground rivers. That's what well diggers look for. They take their giant drills and drill deep into the earth to find the precious water that everyone needs.

Sometimes we judge people because of things we see on the outside. Maybe they walk funny or dress differently or wear their hair in a unique way. Sometimes we forget about all the good that God has put way down deep inside them. They probably feel pretty bad when people misunderstand them and look only on the outside. Maybe you've even had that happen to you. Remember, God has put good things way down deep in each person. Look for those deep things, and you'll find out why everyone is special in God's eyes.

Eatin' Up Everything

Go out to the flock and bring me two choice young goats, so I can prepare some tasty food for your father, just the way he likes it. Genesis 27:9.

Today we hike back to the farm. This time we're looking for goats. As you can see from our verse today, the people of the Bible ate goats. In some places goats are still eaten today. Many people also use goats for garbage duty. That's right, garbage duty! The fact is that goats will eat anything. They'll eat garbage, they'll eat clothes, they'll eat your food, they'll eat anything. It's a wonder they don't get stomachaches more often.

Are you someone who will eat anything? No, I don't mean with your mouth, I mean with your brain. You and I need to be careful what our brain "eats." Satan wants us to make bad choices about the things we watch on TV or look at in magazines; the music we listen to or the people we hang around with. He knows that once something goes into our brain we can't ever get it out. It will always stick in there trying to take our eyes off Jesus. Focus your eyes on Him, and don't be like the goat—just eating up anything you find lying around.

Wrestling With God

When the man saw that he could not overpower him, he touched the socket of Jacob's hip so that his hip was wrenched as he wrestled with the man. Genesis 32:25.

Did you ever think about how it's possible to move your wrist or your arm or your legs or your toes? If it weren't for joints you wouldn't be able to move or hike. Swing your leg at the hip. You can move your leg back and forth, and side to side, can't you? That's because you have a ball-and-socket joint at your hip. Your thighbone is shaped like a ball at the top and fits into a socket, or cup, in your hipbone.

There was a man in the Bible who had a problem with his hip's ball-and-socket joint. His name was Jacob. He had a problem with it because God touched it, and the joint pulled apart. It all happened one night when Jacob was wrestling with God. Why were they wrestling? Because Jacob didn't want to let go until God blessed him.

If you will let God bless you, He will make your life the very best it can be. Ask God to bless you today. Don't let Him go until He does. Wrestle with Him, and He will win your heart, just as He did Jacob's.

Nice to Meet You, Honey

Put some of the best products of the land in your bags and take them down to the man as a gift—a little balm and a little honey, some spices and myrrh, some pistachio nuts and almonds. Genesis 43:11.

Honey, spices, pistachio nuts, and almonds. Sounds pretty good, doesn't it? The men in Genesis 43 were on a hike to visit their brother Joseph—only they didn't know it. You see, they had sold him into slavery many years before, and now he was second in command in Egypt. Of course, Joseph would later tell his brothers who he was, and they had a big family reunion.

Did you notice that one of the things their father sent with them was honey? Do you know where honey comes from? God made honeybees to take the nectar from flower blossoms and turn it into honey.

The main reason people put honey on cereal or use it in baking is that it tastes sweet. And just like honey tastes sweet, God wants you to be a sweet person—someone whom other people like to be around. After all, if people don't want to be around you, how will you tell them about God's love? Stick with God. He'll stick on you and make you as sweet as honey!

18
JANUARY

Brush Those Pearly Whites

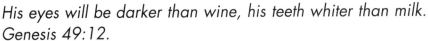

His eyes will be darker than wine, his teeth whiter than milk. Genesis 49:12.

Teeth whiter than milk. Don't you like white teeth? I sure do. It doesn't look very nice if your teeth are yellow and dirty. Yuck! That's exactly why we're hiking to the dentist's office today. Some people don't like to go to the dentist's office. They're afraid of the tools. But the dentist is the person who will help you keep your teeth healthy. You want the dentist on your side.

Genesis 49:12 shows us that even back in Bible times people liked to have their teeth white. Jacob was giving a blessing to his son Judah in this verse. He even blessed his teeth. People like white teeth because it's nicer to smile when your teeth are white and shiny. People often look at people's mouths when they are talking to each other, and it's nice to have a clean, white mouth.

God wants what comes out of our mouths to be clean too. He doesn't want to hear dirty words or stories. He wants to hear kind, sweet words that bless others, just as Jacob blessed Judah. So brush those pearly whites three or four times today, and ask Jesus to help you speak kind, clean words.

Hide and Seek

When she could hide him no longer, she got a papyrus basket for him and coated it with tar and pitch. Then she placed the child in it and put it among the reeds along the bank of the Nile. Exodus 2:3.

Shh. We're hiking by the Nile River today. Be very quiet. Moses' mother has placed him in a papyrus basket and sent him down the river. She didn't want to, but she had to. Read Exodus 2 and find out what happened.

Papyrus is a plant that was used by ancient people to make writing "paper," baskets, and other useful items. People would take strips of the plant and put them side by side. Then they would place another layer of strips over the first layer. Then they beat them carefully with mallets. As they hit them, sap from the plant would run out and act like glue. As the flattened strips lay in the sun, the sap "glue" dried hard and strong. Then the paper was polished with smooth stones and could be written on or used to make baskets.

God makes even the plants He created useful. Imagine how useful He can make you—a live person with a brilliant brain. Let's ask Him today to make us useful and float us right where He needs us.

20 JANUARY

Frogs in Pharaoh's Bed

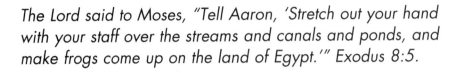

The Lord said to Moses, "Tell Aaron, 'Stretch out your hand with your staff over the streams and canals and ponds, and make frogs come up on the land of Egypt.'" Exodus 8:5.

Tonight we're hiking to the pond. Quietly move to the edge where the tall grass grows. Now, turn on your flashlight! Look. Just on the edge of the water. There's one! Look at him. He's huge! Listen to him. He's loud! He's one of the biggest bullfrogs I've ever seen. He's probably eight inches long. Carefully, scoop him up in your net. Oh, he's gone. They are quick, aren't they? Frogs are such interesting creatures. There are so many different kinds in so many different colors.

Although frogs are really cool, I wouldn't want them everywhere. But that's exactly what happened in Egypt during the plague of the frogs. Frogs were in the sinks, toilets, kitchens, and even in the beds! And all because Pharaoh wouldn't let God's people go.

Pharaoh was so stubborn. He could have avoided so much trouble. Don't you be stubborn. God has so many good things planned for you, but He can trust you with them only if you'll surrender your life to Him. Give your life to Him right now, and keep the frogs out of your bed.

Pickin' Up the Garbage

If you do not let my people go, I will send swarms of flies on you and your officials, on your people and into your houses. The houses of the Egyptians will be full of flies, and even the ground where they are. Exodus 8:21.

Flies! The Egyptians had them all over. Another disgusting plague. Pharaoh sure was stubborn. Why is it that people consider flies to be so disgusting? Are they that ugly? Well, I wouldn't call them handsome, but they're not that ugly. Let's take a hike through fly-infested Egypt to find out.

Oh, no. People are getting very sick. Why? Because flies get into all kinds of garbage and carry diseases everywhere they go. That's why flies are considered so disgusting.

Did you know that some people are like flies? They look for garbage and dirt and rumors in the lives of other people. Then they fly around, light wherever they can, and gossip all that garbage to anyone who will listen. Yuck. The best thing you and I can do is look for the good in other people, not the bad. Once you've found the good, tell everyone you know. Then it's no longer gossip; it's good news.

Bitter and Better!

That same night they are to eat the meat roasted over the fire, along with bitter herbs, and bread made without yeast. Exodus 12:8.

We're hiking into the Israelite camp the night before they hike into the wilderness. On this night the people will eat a special meal. The menu is in our verse for today. One of the things the people were to eat was bitter herbs.

An herb is a plant often used in cooking. Your mother might have containers of parsley or oregano in the cupboard. These are herbs used to make other foods taste better.

The herbs the Israelites ate that night were bitter-tasting. Why would you want to eat anything that is bitter? Couldn't God have allowed them to eat something sweet? No, He wanted them always to remember the hard times they had had in Egypt.

Sometimes it's necessary to do things we really don't like. We might not especially like washing the dishes, but we do want clean ones to eat from. It might be hard to say we're sorry when we've done something wrong, but everyone feels so much better when things are made right. Just remember, if you'll choose to do the bitter things with a good attitude, better things will come to you.

Squished Bread

Celebrate the Feast of Unleavened Bread, because it was on this very day that I brought your divisions out of Egypt. Exodus 12:17.

It was a scary night to hike. The angel of death was passing over every house. If blood wasn't on your doorjamb, the first-born in your family would die. If you had been an Israelite that Passover night, you would have wanted blood on your door.

If you have a Jewish friend you might know that during Passover, Jews still eat unleavened bread. Unleavened bread has no yeast. Yeast is what makes bread rise up nice and fluffy.

Now, you might not want to hear this, but yeast consists of little fungi. When those fungi go to work in the bread dough, they make more and more of themselves and make the bread puffier and puffier.

It really is OK for bread to be puffy, but God doesn't want us to be puffy with pride. Pride causes us to think only of ourselves. God wants us to think of others first.

That night God wanted the Israelites to throw out all their yeast. He wanted them to remember to throw out all their sinfulness. Today, it's OK to keep the yeast when you bake bread, but throw out the sin and pride. That will always be bad for you.

Can I Have a Little Support Here?

Moses took the bones of Joseph with him because Joseph had made the sons of Israel swear an oath. He had said, "God will surely come to your aid, and then you must carry my bones up with you from this place." Exodus 13:19.

Have you ever thought about why you're able to stand up? It's your bones of course. Without your bones, you'd be just a mass of jelly. You would try to move your muscles, but they wouldn't go anywhere because you'd have nothing to hold them up. You and I couldn't even go on our nature hike together if we didn't have bones.

Today's verse tells us that Joseph had asked the Israelites to take his bones with them to the Promised Land. Just like bones give support to the body, Joseph asked his friends and countrymen to give him some support and take his bones to the land flowing with milk and honey.

We can give support to our friends and family too. Just as your bones hold up your body, you can be faithful by holding up your loved ones in prayer and by helping them whenever and wherever they need it. Believe me, they'll appreciate the support.

My Feet Can Run Faster Than Your Horse

The Egyptians pursued them, and all Pharaoh's horses and chariots and horsemen followed them into the sea. Exodus 14:23.

Trudge, trudge, trudge. Here we are hiking through the desert with Moses while the Egyptian army is coming closer and closer. How will we ever escape? Wait, a dark cloud is coming between the Egyptians and us. Moses is stretching out his arm over the Red Sea. Incredible; it's opening! We're walking across on dry land. We're going to make it!

Oh, no! Look! The cloud is lifting and all of Pharaoh's horses and chariots are coming down into the sea on dry land too. I knew this wouldn't work. Hurry! Run . . . We're all across now.

Wait, Moses is stretching out his hand again. Look, all of Pharaoh's army is being sucked under the water! I think I'm happy and sad all at the same time. Happy that we made it safely across, but sad that so many people had to die. It's amazing. Our feet were faster than their horses.

The story of the Israelites crossing the Red Sea shows us that God can accomplish anything—even when we think there's no way out. Never forget to trust in Him. God always has a way to help us.

26 JANUARY

Clean Up Your Act!

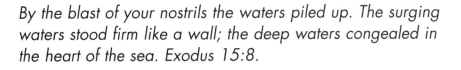

By the blast of your nostrils the waters piled up. The surging waters stood firm like a wall; the deep waters congealed in the heart of the sea. Exodus 15:8.

What a way to describe God's powers. He blew air out of His nostrils, the water stood up, and the Israelites hiked through the Red Sea. Do you think He blew air out of His nose? Well, I guess we don't know for sure, but I think Moses must have been describing what it looked like to him.

Do you know what nostrils are? They are those holes in your nose. Nostrils do something very important we need to understand. They trap dust and dirt. The reason you must clean out your nostrils is that dust and dirt get trapped inside—and that's a good thing. Otherwise, all that dust and dirt would have gone into your lungs.

Did you know that your brain is a filter too? If you've been concentrating on the things of God, your brain tells you very quickly if something you're seeing or hearing isn't good for you. If God's Holy Spirit, working in your brain, tells you that, listen! Keep the dirt of the world from going deep into your soul.

I Wood if I Could

Have them make a chest of acacia wood—two and a half cubits long, a cubit and a half wide, and a cubit and a half high. Exodus 25:10.

As we continue our dusty desert hike with the Israelites, we discover that God had a very special job for Moses to do. He wanted him to choose the very best workers and have them build a special box called the "ark of the covenant." The ark was to be the place that the presence of God Hiimself could be found.

As you can see in today's verse, God wanted the wood-workers to make this box of acacia wood. Acacia wood was from a very special tree. It was the only tree in the desert big enough to build the ark with. God didn't give the men a lot of choices, did He? He asked the workmen to do the best they could with what they had.

Sometimes people make excuses for not doing their best. Some people complain they don't have what it takes to do God's work. God wants us to do our very best with the time and talents He's given us. So don't make excuses—look around you and use what you have to be the best worker for God you can be.

What's in a Name?

Then mount four rows of precious stones on it. In the first row there shall be a ruby, a topaz and a beryl. Exodus 28:17.

It's beautiful. Today we've hiked right into the outer courtyard of the tabernacle in the wilderness. Oh, look! The high priest is here, and look what he's wearing. On his robe is a beautiful, many-colored cloth. On it are 12 of the most beautiful stones I've ever seen in my life. One of them—the third one in the first row—is a beryl.

Beryl is such a beautiful gemstone. It's also a gemstone with many names. If it's slightly bluish-green it's called an emerald, if it's light-blue it's called aquamarine, if it's yellow it's called golden beryl, and if it's colorless beryl it's called goshenite—and there are more names!

Even though it's amazing that the beryl has so many different names, God has even more. The Bible calls God: "the Lord will provide," "the Lord my banner," "the Lord is there," "the Lord send peace," and many, many others. God has so many names because He does so many good things for us. Aren't you glad we have such a multitalented God?

Livin' It Up

Take from this ram the fat, the fat tail, the fat around the inner parts, the covering of the liver, both kidneys with the fat on them, and the right thigh. Exodus 29:22.

Today we've hiked right up to an Israelite sacrifice. All the parts of the ram in our verse today were to be burned on an altar as an offering to God. But why use all those animal parts for the offering—part of its tail, its kidneys, and the covering of its liver? Do you know what a liver does?

The liver is a special organ inside your body that helps clean out poisons. If your liver quits working, the poisons that get into your blood can't be taken out and can kill you. One poison some people put into their body is alcohol. Drinking too much alcohol for too many years can ruin people's livers. The very best solution is never to put alcohol into your body at all.

Just as we shouldn't put poison into our bodies through our mouth, God doesn't want us to put poison into our minds. Our minds are even more sensitive than our livers are. Put only the good things of God into your mind, and you'll find out what real livin' is all about.

Boy, That Smells Good!

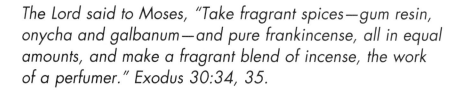

The Lord said to Moses, "Take fragrant spices—gum resin, onycha and galbanum—and pure frankincense, all in equal amounts, and make a fragrant blend of incense, the work of a perfumer." Exodus 30:34, 35.

Wait, do you smell that? I'm a little sweaty after hiking for almost a month, but that's not me I smell. Wait, I know what that is. It's incense. Incense is made from the dried, ground sap of different plants and trees. When it's lit on fire it smells very nice. Well, most of the time.

God asked the high priest to use incense for a very special day called the Day of Atonement. Once a year the high priest went into the Most Holy Place of the tabernacle. That's where the ark rested. It seems that God must have liked the smell of incense, because the priest was to take "fragrant incense" into the Most Holy Place. That means it smelled good.

The Bible compares our prayers to incense in Revelation 8:3. God loves to hear our prayers, just as He loved to smell the fragrant incense. We can always talk to Him in prayer as our friend, but remember, He is also our powerful God. What a great thing it is to have the King of the universe as our very best friend.

Is It or Isn't It?

Then they mounted four rows of precious stones on [the breastpiece]. . . . In the second row a turquoise, a sapphire, and an emerald. Exodus 39:10, 11.

We've learned so much the past four days hiking around the tabernacle in the wilderness. Today we want to learn a little more about the priest's breastpiece. Do you remember it? This was a cloth with beautiful stones that the priest wore on his chest. The very first stone in the second row of the breastpiece was turquoise.

American Indians use turquoise in their jewelry. You may have seen someone with a bright-blue stone in a ring or a bracelet. It may have been turquoise—or maybe not. Turquoise has an impostor called variscite. The only way to tell turquoise and variscite apart is by heating them up. Turquoise and variscite melt at different temperatures. That's the only difference!

How can you tell if you are a true Christian? There's a kind of heat test for Christians, too. When times get hot and things get tough, the true Christian sticks with Jesus. Sure, we all make mistakes, but as we grow closer to Jesus, we'll learn to stick with Him no matter how much Satan heats up His temptations. Stick with Jesus and let Him make you a true gemstone in His crown.

FEBRUARY 1

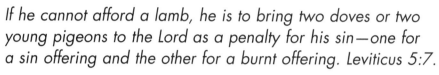

Birds of a Feather Flock Together

If he cannot afford a lamb, he is to bring two doves or two young pigeons to the Lord as a penalty for his sin—one for a sin offering and the other for a burnt offering. Leviticus 5:7.

Can you believe it? We've been hiking for one month now. It's February! I hope you're not too tired, because we have so much more to learn. Today you'll need your binoculars, because we're going bird-watching. Ready? Let's go.

In Bible times when a person sinned they were to bring to the priest a real live animal as an offering. One of the animals that a person could bring was a pure-white dove. Let's find out a little about doves.

You've probably seen doves near your house. Sometimes larger doves are called pigeons. Doves and pigeons like to travel together. You may have seen hundreds of them together in a park.

God wants His people to stick together too. He wants us to care for one another. That's why the disciples formed churches after Jesus left this earth. When you go to church this week, look for someone who needs your help or encouragement. What a difference it will make in their life and yours!

Come On Back In

The son of Aaron who offers the blood and the fat of the fellowship offering shall have the right thigh as his share. Leviticus 7:33.

You really are a hiker! It's been more than a month now and you're still going. You must have very strong legs. Speaking of strong legs—today we're going to talk about one of the reasons your legs are so strong. You have some very strong muscles in the upper part of your leg. This part of your leg is called your thigh. Some of the muscles in your thigh are called adductor muscles.

One of the jobs of the adductor muscles is to bring your leg back to your body. Stand up and balance on one foot. Now swing your other leg as far out to the side as you can. Now bring that leg back in toward your body. The adductor muscles are the ones bringing your leg back toward your body.

God is a little like the adductor muscles He created. He is always trying to bring us closer to Him. We are sinful human beings and often want to swing away from Him, but God never gives up on us. I'm so glad that Jesus never gives up on us and is always inviting us to come to Him, aren't you?

43

All Thumbs

Moses also brought Aaron's sons forward and put some of the blood on the lobes of their right ears, on the thumbs of their right hands and on the big toes of their right feet. Leviticus 8:24.

Oops! We've hiked right into the middle of a special ceremony. Moses is putting drops of blood on Aaron's big toe and thumb. Why would he do that? Thumbs and toes aren't very important parts of the body, are they?

Drop a pencil and pick it up. Did you use your thumb? Now try to pick up that same pencil without using your thumb at all. OK, take off your shoes. Now walk 10 steps without using your big toes. Balance only on the other four toes on each foot. Was it hard to balance?

You can pick up very small objects with your hand easily when you have your thumb to use, and you can run very quickly with great balance when you use your toes. These parts of the body really are very important.

You may think you aren't very important because you're small, but that's not true. You're a very important part of your family and your church. And you're very important to God. So if someone says to you, "You're all thumbs," say, "Thank you very much!"

He's Number One!

His sons brought the blood to him, and he dipped his finger into the blood and put it on the horns of the altar. Leviticus 9:9.

What can your finger do? Well, if you're on a nature hike through the Bible, as we are, it can wrap itself around a walking stick with all its finger friends and help you down the trail. Your finger could be used to pick something up, or it could signal someone to come over to where you are.

If you've ever watched a football game or a baseball game, you might have noticed the fans pointing their index finger to the sky signaling that their team is number one. Really, it doesn't take much to tell everyone which team you are loyal to, does it?

When Aaron put the blood on the altar with his finger, as our verse for today tells us, he was using his finger to point the way to Jesus' sacrifice one day. You and I can use our finger to point others to Jesus too. As we open our Bibles and use our fingers to point out verses that tell others how much God loves them, we're saying our God is number one and we are His best fans ever.

Chew on That for a While

You may eat any animal that has a split hoof completely divided and that chews the cud. Leviticus 11:3.

Well, lookie here! We've hiked right into the barnyard. Would you look at that bovine over there (that's fancy farm talk for cows)? If it ain't just a-chewin' and a-chewin.' Seems like it's a-chewin' forever. That's 'cause it's chewin' its cud. What's a cud, you say? Well, let's just say that a cow chews its food over and over. It chews it so much that by the time the food gets to where it's goin', it's liquid!

Now chewing the cud is a good thing for a cow. It helps the cow digest its food. It needs to chew things over again and again. But you and I don't need to do that with our worries. Sometimes you and I worry about things way too much. We go over and over them before they've even happened. That really is a waste of time and energy. We need to let God take care of our worries. He can watch over us and do the best thing for us. If you'll read 1 Peter 5:7, you'll see exactly what I mean. So don't chew on your worries; let God take care of you—He really can, you know!

Picky, Picky, Picky

These are the birds you are to detest and not eat because they are detestable: . . . the white owl, the desert owl, the osprey. Leviticus 11:13-18.

On today's hike we're bird-watching. Now, I can't imagine eating any of the birds in today's verse, but they are truly amazing to watch. You've probably heard of owls, but maybe not ospreys. Ospreys are big, beautiful birds that are white on the belly, brown on the top, and have a white head with a brown stripe. And they're huge! When the osprey spreads its wings they can reach six feet across. That's taller than many adults! The way the osprey hunts for fish is really cool. It hovers above the water and waits for a fish to come close to the surface. When one does, the osprey jumps in feet-first and grabs the fish.

God created the osprey with the ability to pick fish right out of the water. That's amazing. But you and I need to make sure we don't do that with people. Have you seen anyone you know "hover" over someone until they make a mistake and then pick them apart when they do. God wants us to encourage each other, not discourage. Forgive each other's mistakes and don't be so picky.

Are Ya Heron Me?

These are the birds you are . . . not to eat: . . . the stork, any kind of heron, the hoopoe, and the bat. Leviticus 11:13-19.

On today's hike we're still looking at flying things that God didn't want the Israelites to eat. One of the birds in today's verse is the heron. When I used to live in Florida I would see many great blue herons. They're beautiful blue-gray birds with wingspans of six feet or more.

I think the most beautiful thing about them was the way they flew. They would slowly flap their huge wings and rise gradually into the air. As they left the ground behind they would do a curious thing with their necks. They curved them into the shape of the letter S.

Some people do that with their neck too. No, they don't fly, but they bend their neck in all kinds of weird shapes to hear what someone else is saying. They'll hold their ear up to a door to hear what's being said on the other side, or they'll bend their neck to hear what two people are saying in a private conversation. They just can't seem to mind their own business. Let's you and I not do that. Let's mind our own business and bend our necks to listen to God and what He wants us to know. Are ya heron me?

Katydid Eat an Orange

There are, however, some winged creatures that walk on all fours that you may eat. . . . Of these you may eat any kind of locust, katydid, cricket or grasshopper. Leviticus 11:21, 22.

Listen. Do you hear that buzzing sound as we hike through the tall grass? Get your insect net ready. Now! What'd you get? Look at that. There's a grasshopper. And what's this green thing? It looks a little like a grasshopper, but its head is flat, it's bright green, and its wings look like leaves. I'll tell you what it is. It's a katydid. Now, according to our verse for today, you could eat it, but . . . I don't think so.

There are many kinds of katydids, but today I want to tell you about the fork-tailed bush katydid. These katydids live all over North America. They're very pretty, but the orange growers in California really don't like them. You see, these little pests will destroy oranges by nibbling holes through the skin. Imagine buying an orange in the grocery store with little holes nibbled in it.

Satan is just like the fork-tailed bush katydid in many ways. He tries to take the good that God has made and ruin it. Stay as far away from Satan as possible. Don't let him ruin you like the fork-tailed bush katydid ruins an orange.

Dancing on the Ceiling

Of the animals that move about on the ground, these are unclean for you: . . . the gecko. Leviticus 11:29, 30.

Slowly. Shh. These creatures are very fast. Once they see us, they'll be gone. Look over there—it's an old building. Carefully go through the door. Wow. Did you see that? It ran right across the top of the ceiling. It's a gecko. Geckos have tiny hairs on the bottom of their feet that will grab on to anything. Geckos can run up walls, across ceilings, and anywhere else they want to go. If you didn't know about those little hairs on their feet, running across the ceiling would seem like a miracle. It would seem impossible.

Many times in our lives there seem to be impossible things we have to do. Maybe our mom or dad just can't seem to find a job or maybe our schoolwork seems extra tough. We just don't see how the job can be done.

Remember this. God can do anything. He really can do the impossible. The next time you face a job that seems like it can't be done, remember the gecko and ask God to help you through. He loves you so much, He'll "run across the ceiling" to show you how much.

Dragon Slayer

Of the animals that move about on the ground, these are unclean for you: . . . the monitor lizard. Leviticus 11:29, 30.

Today we're hiking right through Leviticus 11:30 again. There are so many wonderful animals there we just had to stop for a while. Today we talk about the monitor lizard. Most monitor lizards are huge. The Komodo dragon, a type of monitor lizard, can grow up to 10 feet long. That's taller than the ceiling in most people's houses. The Komodo dragon lives on the island of Komodo in Indonesia. You may want to look at a map of the world and discover where Indonesia is. Komodo dragons are carnivores. That means they eat meat. They are ferocious killers. When they find their prey they use their very sharp teeth to serve up dinner.

There's another dragon talked about in the Bible. Revelation 20:2 tells us that Satan is the real dragon. He's ferocious too. He's out to put an end to you and me. But don't worry. Revelation tells us that God will chain him up, and finally, when heaven comes to earth he will never bother us again. I'm so glad that our God is so much more powerful than the Komodo dragon and the real dragon, aren't you?

11 FEBRUARY

True Colors

Of the animals that move about on the ground, these are unclean for you: . . . the chameleon. Leviticus 11:29, 30.

Here we are hiking through Leviticus 11:30 again. God sure did fill these verses with lots of animals. Today's special animal is another lizard. It's the chameleon. These lizards are one of the very coolest. Their secret—shh, don't tell anyone—is that they can change colors. If they're sitting on a brown rock they turn brown, if they're sitting on a green leaf they turn green, if they're sitting on gray tree bark, they turn gray. God gave them this special ability so they can hide from other animals that might eat them.

Even though it's a very good thing that the chameleon can turn different colors it's not a good thing for you and me. No, I don't mean your skin might turn colors; I mean you shouldn't change who you are for different people. You and I should always stand up for Jesus no matter who we are with. Even if someone makes fun because we obey God, we should always be happy to witness for Him.

Don't be like the chameleon, which changes into something else wherever it happens to be. Be God's child every day and around everyone—a boy or girl who loves Jesus and isn't afraid to show their true colors.

Brave Little Soldiers

The priest is to examine the sore on his skin, and if the hair in the sore has turned white and the sore appears to be more than skin deep, it is an infectious skin disease. Leviticus 13:3.

Ouch! I don't like it when I get cuts and scrapes and they get infected and turn all white and gooey. Do you know why sores sometimes turn white? Let's hike right to the doctor's tent and find out why. Doc says when a sore gets white, the body has sent out its little soldiers, the white blood cells. They are trying very hard to fight the dirt that has entered the cut in your body. Your white blood cells shoot "bullets" called antibodies that try to kill the germs that are making you sick or making your cut very sore. If you didn't have white blood cells, you would be very sick all the time and would eventually die.

Satan wants to hurt us. He doesn't want us to be friends with God. He wants to put sin's infection into our minds and makes us "sin sick." We must fight back by sticking close to Dr. Jesus. Read God's Word and talk to Him every day so that sin's infection won't keep you from enjoying your friendship with Jesus.

Scrub the Tub

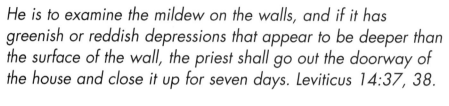

He is to examine the mildew on the walls, and if it has greenish or reddish depressions that appear to be deeper than the surface of the wall, the priest shall go out the doorway of the house and close it up for seven days. Leviticus 14:37, 38.

Mildew. It can be many different colors. It grows in dark, damp places. It can even grow in your bathroom. It's yucky. Mildew is a type of fungus.

As we've hiked into the Israelite camp today we see the priest examining the wall of someone's house. He's found mildew. Back then God said if the mildew was found in a house, everyone was to leave for a week. If you find mildew in your bathtub today, you don't need to leave your house. We have powerful cleaners that destroy mildew.

In ancient times God wanted His people to stay clean and free of disease. He wanted them to stay away from things like mildew. Mildew grows like sin. If even a little sin is found in our lives, we need to turn to Jesus to clean it up. We don't want it to grow and keep us from seeing Jesus clearly each day. So scrub your tub and keep it clean. Then read Psalm 51:1, 2. It will tell you how to keep your heart clean.

Leave It Alone

These are the regulations for . . . an itch. Leviticus 14:54.

Scratch, scratch, scratch. Itch, itch, itch. If you've ever been on a real hike, you've probably spent some time scratching a bug bite or a poison ivy rash or a beesting. Obviously, the Israelites had an itch or two themselves, according to our verse for the day. You see, when a mosquito bites you or a poisonous plant rubs against your leg, it puts poison on or under your skin. This poison or venom makes your skin itch. When you scratch, it can get all red and infected. Your mom or dad has probably told you to leave it alone. It's hard not to scratch something that itches so much, isn't it?

Sometimes there are things in life we need to leave alone, too. There are things we just shouldn't touch. Dishonesty is one of those things. It seems like one small lie leads to another, which leads to another, which leads to another. It's best never to tell that first lie. Just as we need to stay away from the itch and never scratch it in the first place, stay away from dishonesty and never tell that first lie. Believe me, you'll be much healthier for it.

15 FEBRUARY

Hey, It's Cold Out Here!

Command the Israelites to bring you clear oil of pressed olives for the light so that the lamps may be kept burning continually. Leviticus 24:2.

When the Israelites were hiking through the desert, God told them to keep the lamps in the tabernacle burning at all times. The Israelites used oil-burning lamps. God told them to use olive oil in these lamps.

Do you know where olive oil comes from? In Bible times special presses were made from two flat pieces of wood. The olives were squished between the two boards. The harder the olives were pressed, the more oil came out.

The funny thing about olives is that in order for them to grow, it has to be pretty cold for two or three months of the year. If the temperature doesn't reach about 44 degrees Fahrenheit each day for at least a couple of months, olives won't grow. Fortunately, the weather was just right for the Israelites.

Sometimes God takes us through "cold" hard times, just like olive trees. He wants us to grow the fruit of the Spirit—things like joy and kindness and patience. So when He takes you through difficult times, don't ask to have them taken away. Ask God to help you grow the "fruit" you need to be a better person for Him.

It's Too Crowded!

If a man dedicates to the Lord part of his family land, its value is to be set according to the amount of seed required for it. Leviticus 27:16.

Careful, don't step on the plants with those big hiking boots of yours. Did you know that in order to plant a field of barley, or any other plant, you must have just the right amount of seed?

If you put too little seed on the field, you wouldn't have much of a crop. But how could you ever put too much seed on? If you completely covered the ground with seed, your field would soon be blanketed with little plants. They'd be so thick, it would be like carpet in the living room. It would look nice for a while, but as those little plants grew up they would get more and more crowded until they wouldn't have any more room to grow and would eventually die.

When you try to crowd too many things into your life, you can actually crowd Jesus right out. He wants us to be happy people who do lots of interesting things, but He would be very sad if we were so busy we didn't have time for Him. Don't crowd Him out. Take time each day with Him and develop into a healthy, growing Christian.

True North

On the north will be the divisions of the camp of Dan, under their standard. The leader of the people of Dan is Ahiezer son of Ammishaddai. Numbers 2:25.

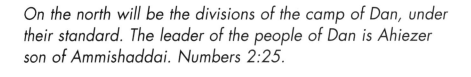

Today we're hiking into the Israelite camp. It's huge. There are close to 2 million people. How will we know where to go? Fortunately, the Bible tells us the camp of Dan is to the north. Do you know how to tell where north is?

If you have a compass you will see the needle always points north. It points to the north because earth is like a big magnet. It draws the needle to the north every time. But here's the tricky part—there are actually two norths. That's right! The area where the compass needle points is called magnetic north. It's about 1,000 miles from the North Pole, called true north, where the actual top of the world is. That means your compass isn't actually pointing to true north.

It's hard to believe that you can't trust your compass completely, isn't it? It's also true that you can't trust your feelings completely, either. You might not feel like praying or reading God's Word, but that's probably the time when you need to do those things most. Focus on Jesus, our true north. He'll always lead you safely home.

Do You Have Thick Skin?

They are to take all the articles used for ministering in the sanctuary, wrap them in a blue cloth, cover that with hides of sea cows and put them on a carrying frame. Numbers 4:12.

Have you ever heard of a sea cow? Do you think it's a four-legged creature that eats grass, makes milk, and lives in the sea? No, not quite. Actually, it's an animal that looks a little like a seal and a little like a whale and lives in shallow water. Their thick skin protects them from the water they live in. God told the Israelites to use the hides of the sea cows to cover parts of the sanctuary. That was a great idea, because sea-cow hides are very protective.

Sometimes we need "thick skin" just like the sea cow. No, that doesn't mean we need to grow more skin. It means when people do or say things to hurt us, we need to ask God to help us be courageous and pray for that person instead of thinking so much about the hurt. Let's be sea cows and start praying for God's love to cover those who don't treat us very well.

19 FEBRUARY

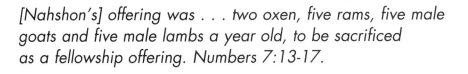

Nahshon Had a Little Lamb

[Nahshon's] offering was . . . two oxen, five rams, five male goats and five male lambs a year old, to be sacrificed as a fellowship offering. Numbers 7:13-17.

Quiet now. We've hiked to the tabernacle in the Israelite camp again. It's Nahshon's turn to bring his offering. Why did Nahshon have to sacrifice all those animals, and especially a little lamb? The poor lambs were only a year old.

The reason God said a lamb must die was to help the Israelites understand that sin is a terrible thing—so terrible that it would cause the death of one of His innocent creatures. But it wasn't a lamb that paid for the Israelites' sins. All those lambs sacrificed so long ago were all pointing to Jesus, the Lamb of God, who died on the cross.

The reason we don't have to sacrifice lambs today is that Jesus, God's Lamb, already died 2.000 years ago. That was the most terrible sacrifice of all. But it's also very good. Because Jesus did that for us, you and I can live with Him right now in our hearts, and very soon in heaven forever. It's very sad that little lambs had to die, but I'm glad the Lamb of God died for us, aren't you?

Be a Cucumber, Not a Sour Pickle

We remember the fish we ate in Egypt at no cost—also the cucumbers. Numbers 11:5.

The Israelites were tired of hiking in the desert after just a few days. In fact, they were complaining about it to Moses. Do you think the Israelites should have been complaining? God had given them food to eat. They weren't starving. But as you can see in our verse for today, they were complaining that they didn't have the good vegetables they ate in Egypt.

One of those vegetables was the cucumber. Think of how tasty and refreshing a cucumber is. They're so delicious when you pick them right out of the garden, cool them off a little bit, peel them, and eat them. I guess we can see why the Israelites were remembering the tasty cucumber. But instead of thinking about what they didn't have, maybe the Israelites should have been thinking about what they did have.

They weren't slaves anymore! They didn't have to worship the Egyptian gods! They had God to lead them in a pillar of fire, and they were headed to the Promised Land! We could think about all the things we don't have, but God wants us to remember all the good things we do have. Count your blessings today—be a cucumber, not a sour pickle.

21 FEBRUARY

Vegetable Overboard!

We remember the fish we ate in Egypt at no cost—also the . . . leeks. Numbers 11:5.

We're hiking through the desert. We see a lake—yes, sometimes you'll find lakes in the desert. You're about to hike around the big lake when you see a boat. You're so glad to see the boat—now you won't have to walk around the lake. You run over to the boat, only to discover it's full of leeks. Should you: Bail out the water and row quickly to the other side, give up on the boat and walk around the lake, or sit down in the boat and have lunch? Well, are we talking about l-e-e-k-s or l-e-a-k-s? A leak is a hole that water could come through—a leek is a vegetable that belongs to the lily family and tastes like a very sweet onion. People cook leeks and eat them with boiled potatoes and other foods. Leeks make other foods taste better.

You can make life better, just like the leek makes food better. By being a kind, loving person you can help the people around you be happier and more thankful for the good things God has given them. So don't be the leak that sinks the boat; be the leek that makes life taste better for everyone.

Whoa, That's Strong!

We remember the fish we ate in Egypt at no cost—also the . . . onions. Numbers 11:5.

Today, as we continue our hike through the garden, we've come to a rather strong-smelling patch of vegetables. It's the onions! Now, you may not have known this, but not all onions are the same. Some taste very sweet and mild, some taste very strong and spicy. Some don't make your breath taste too bad, some will make everyone move away from you. Some people think onions make food taste good; other people think onions make food taste bad.

You can also be like an onion. When someone is doing something you don't like, you can ask him or her to stop in different ways. If someone is using bad language you could say, "Hey, buddy, close your trap. I don't want to hear it anymore." Or you could nicely say, "Excuse me, but I was wondering if you would not use that language." Saying hard things nicely is called being tactful. When it comes to onions, use whichever ones you like. But when it comes to talking with others, be a sweet, tactful onion, not a strong, spicy one. Others will think you taste delightful.

Strong Medicine

We remember the fish we ate in Egypt at
no cost—also the . . . garlic. Numbers 11:5.

Have you ever eaten garlic bread? M-m-m, delicious. At least I think so. Until I met my father-in-law, I thought the only way to make garlic bread was to mix garlic salt with butter and spread it on bread. But then I found out how "real" garlic bread is made. My father-in-law takes tough European bread and fries it in oil. Then he takes a fresh chunk of garlic and rubs it into the bread. Talk about strong!

Garlic isn't just for bread, though. I have a friend who takes garlic pills to stay healthy. Scientists have discovered that garlic may prevent cancer. What wonderful things garlic can do; it tastes great and can help heal diseases. God really is the great physician, and vegetables are some of His medicines.

It's important to eat right and stay healthy. But don't do it just so you can play games and have lots of energy. Do it because a quick mind and body can think well and hear God best. So eat your veggies and look for God to show you how to live. He'll talk if you're listening.

What Is It?

The manna was like coriander seed and looked like resin. Numbers 11:7.

We've been hiking with the Israelites a long time now. I've decided there's a lot of complaining going on around here. We've been talking about vegetables so much the past few days because the children of Israel are tired of manna. They want the vegetables they had in Egypt. Well, I can understand why they want tasty vegetables. They're good for you and they're delicious. But I think we should be thankful for the manna, don't you? What's manna, you say?

Manna is a Hebrew word that means "What is it?" It was called that because when it fell from heaven the Israelites said, "What is it?" God gave it to them at the beginning of this desert hike. Joshua 5:12 says it stopped as soon as the people moved into the Promised Land and started to eat food that grew there. God's timing is perfect. God always knows what to do and when to do it. Sometimes we get impatient and complain to God about things, but we need to remember that God knows everything—we don't. So let's be patient. Remember the manna, and with God in control of our lives, we have nothing to worry about.

Be Careful What You Say!

Now a wind went out from the Lord and drove quail in from the sea. It brought them down all around the camp to about three feet above the ground, as far as a day's walk in any direction. Numbers 11:31.

Quail! There're all kinds of them—three feet of them, to be exact. But we'll get back to that story later. Quail are birds you'll find in many places of the world. Today I want to tell you about one kind of quail called a bobwhite. Bob is a beautiful little bird with multicolored feathers. He's called a bobwhite because he goes around saying "Bob White, Bob White" all day. No kidding, I've heard them, and that's exactly what they sound like.

You see, Bob is known by what comes out of his mouth. You're judged by the words that come out of your mouth too. Are they kind, loving words, or are they mean, hateful words? Are they words of truth or words of dishonesty?

The Israelites were known as complainers because complaining often came out of their mouths. They were tired of manna and they wanted meat to eat, so God gave it to them— all three feet of it. Watch what comes out of your mouth. You might be surprised what you get.

Big Blessings

When they reached the Valley of Eshcol, they cut off a branch bearing a single cluster of grapes. Two of them carried it on a pole between them, along with some pomegranates and figs. Numbers 13:23.

Read the verse for today carefully. We're hiking with two men who have cut off a single cluster of grapes and strung them up on a pole between them. These were some mighty big grapes.

Today there are some pretty big fruits and vegetables still being grown. In 2001 the biggest pumpkin on record was 1,262 pounds. Imagine trying to get all the pumpkin seeds out of that one. The biggest apple ever grown was 3 pounds 11 ounces, and the biggest squash ever grown weighed in at 1,064 pounds. Amazing!

Although the fruit in the Promised Land was huge, and even though there are still gigantic fruits and veggies still being grown, they're nothing compared to the things that God has waiting for you and me in heaven. Read what Paul wrote in 1 Corinthians 2:9. Talk about big blessings. Those will be the biggest.

27 FEBRUARY

Burned Up for God

Tell Eleazar son of Aaron, the priest, to take the censers out of the smoldering remains and scatter the coals some distance away, for the censers are holy. Numbers 16:37.

Today we've hiked right into an ancient Israelite worship service, and they're burning things. In the verse above we see that the priests had censers, which were special bowls made of gold. The priests put sweet-smelling incense in them to represent the people's prayers rising up to God. The incense didn't usually burn completely, and coals were left.

When wood is not burned completely it also leaves coals. Maybe you've helped build a campfire. If your fire didn't burn the wood completely, you were left with blackened coals. The charcoal left over can be used for many things. It can be burned again at very high temperatures and used to put a hard shell on the outside of certain metals. It can be ground up and taken by mouth to settle upset stomachs. It can be used as an ingredient in gunpowder, and it's even used to take the bad-tasting stuff out of drinking water.

Even when people think we aren't very good at some things, God can use us to do great things for Him. Don't let anybody cause you to believe that your life is worthless. If God can make use of leftover, half-burned wood, He can certainly use you and me with all our mistakes to help people learn about Him.

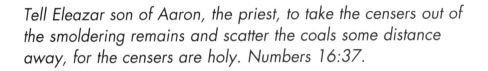

Clean as a Whistle

After that, the priest must wash his clothes and bathe himself with water. He may then come into the camp. Numbers 19:7.

Numbers 19:7 tells us the priest had to clean up with water after making special sacrifices. Water is such an amazing thing. Most of the earth is covered by it. Your body is mostly water. A tomato is almost all water. You need it on the inside to clean you out, and you need it on the outside to clean you up. In some places you can find it just a few inches below the ground's surface, and in some places you must dig hundreds of feet down to get it. It makes plants grow and falls out of the sky. Next to air, it's the thing your body needs most. You can live only about four days without it. Yes, water is very important.

Just like water is necessary for you to live, forgiveness, which comes from God, is necessary for you to live eternally. Without forgiveness, you and I could not spend forever with Jesus. It cleanses your heart of sin and makes you feel so good all over. Ask Jesus to forgive your sins right now and find out how good it feels to be washed with forgiveness.

Aloe, I Can Help

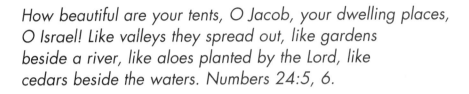

How beautiful are your tents, O Jacob, your dwelling places, O Israel! Like valleys they spread out, like gardens beside a river, like aloes planted by the Lord, like cedars beside the waters. Numbers 24:5, 6.

How God must have loved His people! He even liked the looks of their tents; thousands and thousands of them all lined up. They looked like "aloes planted by the Lord."

Do you know what aloe is? It's obviously a plant, but aloe isn't just your average plant. People many years ago discovered that if you break an aloe leaf open and put its gooey juice on a skin burn, the burn would heal very quickly. As we hike through the desert with the Israelites, we see them picking aloe plants for their injuries. Even today, some people grow aloe in their homes to use as medicine for burns.

God's Holy Spirit is a lot like aloe. The Bible calls Him the Comforter. When we are sad or discouraged, He will come into our hearts and minds and let us know that Jesus is taking care of everything. He lets us know we don't have to worry. I'm glad the Holy Spirit can spread His love all over us and heal us from the burns that we sometimes get from life.

Purifying Fire

Then Eleazar the priest said to the soldiers who had gone into battle, "This is the requirement of the law that the Lord gave Moses: Gold, silver, bronze, iron, tin, lead and anything else that can withstand fire must be put through the fire, and then it will be clean." Numbers 31:21-23.

Gold, silver, bronze, iron, tin, and lead. What are all these things? If you said metals, you were right. Your car, your refrigerator, your bathtub, and your spoons are all made of metal.

Even though your spoons and forks are bright and shiny now, the metal they were made from didn't look that bright and shiny when it was dug from the earth. It had many other materials mixed with it. As we hike into the Israelite camp today, we see metalworkers getting the impurities out of metal. How did they do it? With fire! When metal is put in very hot fire all the other materials flow away.

That's what God wants to do with our lives. He wants the bad stuff to flow away from us. But we can't do that ourselves. What we must do is decide to give our lives to Him. If we'll do that, He'll do the rest. Let's ask God to make us pure, holy, and shiny for Him today.

Look in the Sky, It's a . . .

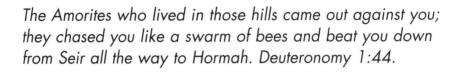

The Amorites who lived in those hills came out against you; they chased you like a swarm of bees and beat you down from Seir all the way to Hormah. Deuteronomy 1:44.

Swarm. For some people, even the word sounds scary. Imagine having a swarm of bees after you. We've hiked right into one of the saddest moments in Israel's history. Because they didn't obey God, the Amorites came out of the hills like a swarm of bees and defeated Israel in battle. Ouch.

Have you ever seen a swarm of bees? No, I don't mean 20 or 30 bees. I mean more like 20,000 or 30,000. When bees swarm, they really swarm! One of the jobs swarming bees have is protecting their queen. She's the leader—she's the one who will start a new colony. If you've seen bees swarm, the queen may have been in the middle.

When Jesus comes again it will look a little like a swarm of bees. They won't be bees surrounding Him, though; they'll be angels. Those angels will shout and sing for joy because you and I will finally be coming to heaven with them. I run *from* swarming bees, but I want to run *to* the heavenly swarm. Won't you run with me?

Hot Sand, Cool Feet

He led you through the vast and dreadful desert, that thirsty and waterless land, with its venomous snakes and scorpions. Deuteronomy 8:15.

Have you ever been in the middle of a desert? If you have, you know that a desert is a dry, lonely place. In fact, deserts lose more water through evaporation than they gain through snow or rain. That means deserts get drier and drier as the years go by.

We've been hiking with the Israelites for a couple of months now, but can you imagine what it would have been like to hike with them for 40 years? That's exactly what the Israelites did, simply because they didn't believe God would lead them into the very comfortable Promised Land of Israel. But God did an amazing thing for His people even though they didn't believe Him. You can read about it in Deuteronomy 8:4. With all that hiking, the people's sandals never wore out and their feet never did swell—not even once in 40 years.

You see, God loves you so much He'll even take care of you when you disobey or don't believe Him. He's a very loving God. Believe His promises today and enter into the Promised Land of heaven when He comes to take us home.

The Hard Rock Café

He brought you water out of hard rock. Deuteronomy 8:15.

Have you ever heard of the Hard Rock Café? It's a restaurant. Well, today we've hiked right into the very first Hard Rock Café. Today's verse tells us that God brought water out of a rock for the Israelites. Imagine that! The Israelites had a cool, refreshing drink right there in the desert.

Hard rock. Does that make you curious? Wouldn't you think all rocks were hard? Well, I guess most are pretty hard, but some rocks are harder than others. For instance, sandstone is softer than obsidian. Sandstone is really sand and quartz glued together. It's soft enough to be carved. Obsidian is volcanic glass. Below the surface of the earth is hot liquid that comes from volcanoes. As it cools, it forms volcanic glass. If the chemicals are just right, it can form obsidian. Obsidian is very hard.

What are you like? Are you letting God carve you into the person He wants you to be? Or are you hard like obsidian? Be soft for God today and let Him create a beautiful likeness of Him out of your life.

Honey Shampoo

Observe therefore all the commands I am giving you today,
. . . so that you may live long in the land that the Lord swore
to your forefathers to give to them and their descendants,
a land flowing with milk and honey. Deuteronomy 11:8, 9.

Imagine diving into a river that was filled with honey instead of water. What a sticky mess that would be! Imagine the time your mother would have washing your bathing suit. What a disaster!

God promised His people a special land they could hike right into. He said this land was flowing with milk and honey. Do you think that means there was honey in the rivers and milk in the lakes? No, not really. Milk and honey were some of the favorite foods in Bible times. What God meant was that the land He was giving them had the best of everything.

Did you know that God wants to give you the best of everything, too? He does! Oh, that doesn't mean you'll get everything you want. What it does mean is that God will give us peace and make us happy because He's living in us. Won't you give your life to Him today? He'll give you a life flowing with milk and honey. And you won't even have sticky hair!

Flyin' Underwater

You may eat any clean bird. But these you may not eat: . . . the cormorant. Deuteronomy 14:11-17.

Did you see that? A bird, or something, flew up and out of the water. It was big! It must have been three feet long. It had a fish in its bill too. Hey, it had a bill, so it must have been a bird, right?

We've hiked right up to the seacoast today, and what we saw was a cormorant. Try to say cormorant five times fast. Cormorants are fascinating birds that live where there's water and fish to eat. The way they do it is great. They'll swim on top of the water, find a fish, and then dive in. That's right, they dive into the water—and then they swim until they get their fish. Now, that's sticking with something until you get it.

In Matthew 4:19 Jesus said He would make His disciples fishers of men. And just like the cormorant, Jesus wants us to go wherever we need to fish for men. He wants us to stick with it and not give up on our friends and neighbors. He wants us to dive as many times as we need to bring others to Him. And when we bring our friends to Jesus, we'll be so happy we'll fly like a cormorant.

Don't Get Your Feathers Up

You may eat any clean bird. But these you may not eat: . . . the stork, any kind of heron, the hoopoe and the bat. Deuteronomy 14:11-18.

We're hiking, hiking, bird-watching, bird-watching. Ah, yes. There's a stork, there's a heron, there's a hoopoe, and there's a bat. OK, God said don't eat, so we won't. Wait a minute. Did you say hoopoe? What's a hoopoe? Everything else in that verse flies, so it might be safe to say it flies. Did you say you think it's a bird? Well, you're right.

Hoopoes are pretty birds. They're pinkish-brown on the head with black-and-white-striped wings. The prettiest thing about them is their crest, a group of feathers that can stick straight up on the top of their head.

There's a saying that goes, "Don't get your feathers up." It means calm down and don't get so upset. In other words, think things through. The Bible tells us that patience is a fruit of the Spirit. Follow God's advice. Don't eat a hoopoe, and don't be like one either. When you're upset, stop and think things through. Don't fly off angry.

Duck, Quick!

You may eat any clean bird. But these you may not eat: . . . the bat. Deuteronomy 14:11-18.

The sun has just gone down, but there's still light in the sky. Are those birds? No, I don't think so. They fly . . . differently. They dart back and forth like they're trying to get away from something. As we hike in the early evening with the Israelites all the little children are watching these creatures. Do you know what they are? That's right; they're bats.

Bats help people by eating insects. If they didn't, we'd have so many insects that they'd be everywhere, all the time. And they're not trying to get away from anything. They actually bounce sound waves off the little insects. When the sound waves bounce back they know where the insect is, and they dart over and eat it. If it weren't for those sound waves, the bat wouldn't be able to find their dinner in the dark.

God's Holy Spirit is like that in a way. He can help us find a person who needs our help. We might walk right by someone who needs cheering up, but the Holy Spirit can show us we need to stop and talk for a while. Tune in to Jesus today. He'll help you find people in need, faster than the bat finds bugs.

Juicy Fruits

When you lay siege to a city for a long time, fighting against it to capture it, do not destroy its trees by putting an ax to them, because you can eat their fruit. Do not cut them down. Deuteronomy 20:19.

Don't you just love to eat a fresh juicy pear, or a crisp delicious apple, or a luscious orange—the kind that squirts little streams of orange juice on your cheeks when you bite into it? Is your mouth watering yet? Have you ever eaten fresh fruit right off the tree? It's so good!

That's why God told the Israelites not to cut down fruit trees when they attacked their enemies. He wanted them to save the trees so they could eat the fruit. God knew they needed the vitamins in fruit, just like you do.

Did you know that God is interested in every part of your life, even in the food you eat? He is. He loves you that much! Do you have some fruit in the house right now? If you do, and it's all right with Mom and Dad, go get some right now, kneel down, and thank God for the delicious fruit He made and then chow down. God's happy when you enjoy the good things He's given you.

11 MARCH

Hold Back Those Hoppers

You will sow much seed in the field but you will harvest little, because locusts will devour it. Deuteronomy 28:38.

Have you ever caught a grasshopper? It was hard to catch, wasn't it? If you were fast enough to catch one, did you see the big pincers on its mouth? Grasshoppers use those pincers to eat lots of food. If you have them around your garden, they'll sometimes eat leaves from your vegetable plants. One grasshopper can eat a lot! Imagine that you doubled the size of the grasshopper you caught and put millions of them in your garden. In just a few minutes your garden would be gone!

That's what Deuteronomy 28:38 is talking about. These big, hungry grasshoppers were called locusts . . . and we've just hiked into a swarm. If God's people would only put their trust in Him and obey Him, He could protect them. But if the people left God's protection, they wouldn't be able to harvest many crops; the locusts would eat them all.

God doesn't want us to hurt. But if we choose to walk away from God, we're really saying we don't want His protection. I don't want to be out of God's protection, do you? Let's hop into His arms today. He'll keep us safe!

Sulfur or Sailing?

The whole land will be a burning waste of salt and sulfur—nothing planted, nothing sprouting, no vegetation growing on it. It will be like the destruction of Sodom and Gomorrah. Deuteronomy 29:23.

Wow, we've hiked into a scary place—a burning waste of salt and sulfur. I see why there isn't anything growing here. Sulfur is a yellow rock that burns very quickly. That's why Sodom and Gomorrah burned up so quickly. The Bible says in Genesis 19:24 that sulfur rained down on the city and burned it up.

Sodom and Gomorrah were destroyed because of sin. The cities had become so wicked that God knew He must destroy them. He didn't want to destroy them, and He gave people a chance to escape. But sin finally destroyed those cities.

Just like sulfur burns, sin does too. God wants us to stay as far away from sin as possible. Someday He will have to destroy the earth again. That will be the day He comes to take those who love Him to heaven. He doesn't want us to be caught in sin and sulfur. Don't worry, though—as long as you love Him and stick with Him, you won't be caught in the sulfur. You'll be sailing through the sky on your way to glory.

13 MARCH

Help, I'm Falling!

He guarded [Jacob] . . . like an eagle that stirs up its nest and hovers over its young, that spreads its wings to catch them and carries them on its pinions. Deuteronomy 32:10, 11.

One day I saw the most amazing thing. I was hiking through a wilderness area when I saw an eagle standing in her nest. The eagle was doing something with her feet. Soon the eagle had pushed her baby right to the edge of the nest. Then with one swift kick the eagle booted her baby right out of the nest!

Then all of a sudden the mother eagle hopped out of the nest and started diving toward the falling baby eagle. "Hurry," I said! "Save your baby." The mother eagle swooped right past the baby eagle, spread her wings out wide, and caught the baby eagle on the tops of her wings. I found out that's how a baby eagle learns to fly.

Sometimes you and I need to be taught lessons. Sometimes they're scary lessons. But if you and I are trusting in Jesus, we know He'll always take care of us like the mother eagle took care of her baby. We may not always like the ways God uses to teach us, but if we pay attention, soon He'll have us flying, too—flying through life and trusting in Him.

You're the Cheesiest

He nourished [Jacob] with curds and milk from herd and flock and with fattened lambs and goats, with choice rams of Bashan and the finest kernels of wheat. Deuteronomy 32:13, 14.

Curds and milk—where have we hiked today? Well, we're on an Israelite farm with goats and cows and sheep. Our verse for today tells how God took care of Jacob when he was running from Esau. One of the things that God gave him was curds and milk.

If you were to milk a goat like the Israelites did, and let the milk sit for a short time, little, solid, fatty chunks—or curds—would rise to the top. The people would take the curds and make cheese and drink the milk that was left. It doesn't sound very yummy, but that's what they did, and they thought it was delicious.

Yes, the curds rose to the top. Sometimes—I'm not sure why—people want to say bad things about us. But don't let others' meanness turn you into a mean person. Always be kind and true to Jesus, and like curds in goat's milk, you'll rise to the top. You'll be the cheesiest. And just maybe those who aren't so kind will see your example and want to be the cheesiest too!

Make the Snake Run!

Their wine is the venom of serpents, the deadly poison of cobras. Deuteronomy 32:33.

Watch out and make sure you have your hiking boots on today. We're hiking into the land of the cobra. When God talked about the deadly poison of cobras, He knew exactly what He was talking about.

Cobras are very deadly snakes. They live in parts of Africa, Australia, and Asia. Cobras are famous for spreading the rib bones in their neck and making a "hood." It looks very scary.

The Indian cobra kills several thousand people each year because it sneaks into a house at night looking for rats and accidentally runs into the owner. The cobra gets scared and bites the owner.

But even though the cobra is deadly, it can be "tamed," in a way. Snake charmers play their flutes to make cobras spread their neck and "dance." Amazingly, they make those deadly snakes do whatever they want them to.

Satan is powerful. But did you know you can make Satan do what you want, just like the snake charmers make the cobra do what they want? Read about it in James 4:7. You can make the devil run. As powerful as Satan is, God and you together are much stronger.

Watch Out!

About Dan he said: "Dan is a lion's cub, springing out of Bashan." Deuteronomy 33:22.

Just before the Israelites crossed over the Jordan River into the Promised Land, Moses gave special blessings to each of Israel's tribes. In Moses' blessings he described the tribe of Dan as "a lion's cub, springing out of Bashan." Let's hike with them today and find out what God was talking about.

If you've ever visited a zoo, you've see plenty of signs that tell you to stay away from the animals' cages and pens. Why do they tell us to stay away? Those little lion cubs are so cuddly. It wouldn't hurt to pet one, would it? Yes, it would! Many people have been hurt badly and some even killed because they walked up to a baby lion or bear in the wild. Why? Because the mother was waiting nearby and came out to defend her cub. The unsuspecting person didn't realize that mama was around.

Satan is like that too. He throws his temptations right out in front of us. If we reach out to take or touch or do something we shouldn't, he's right there waiting to pounce on us. Stay as far away from Satan and his temptations as possible, and God will protect you.

17 MARCH

Secret Agent Man

(She had taken them up to the roof and hidden them under the stalks of flax she had laid out on the roof.). Joshua 2:6.

Did you ever play spy? I did, and my two sons still love to. Hiding behind buildings, talking on walkie-talkies, and running away from the invisible enemy is so much fun. In today's verse these spies were for real. God had sent them into the Promised Land to check things out. Soon someone was after them, so they ran into a woman's house and asked her to hide them. She took them up to the roof and covered them with flax.

Flax is a plant that stands three or four feet tall. People, even today, still make clothes from it. That's right, clothes from a plant. Very fine, long-lasting shirts, pants, and tablecloths are made from flax.

Matthew 6:28, 29 says that even Solomon wasn't clothed as beautifully as the lilies of the field. Jesus meant we shouldn't worry about our clothes or anything else. If God can show people how to make clothes out of flax, and cover His spies with it, you and I should stay worry-free. God's taking care of us and covering us with the best clothes of all—His robe of righteousness!

Pass the Salt, Please

The water from upstream stopped flowing. It piled up in a heap a great distance away, at a town called Adam in the vicinity of Zarethan, while the water flowing down to the Sea of the Arabah (the Salt Sea) was completely cut off. So the people crossed over opposite Jericho. Joshua 3:16.

What a miracle in today's verse! As we hike with the Israelites today, we see God pile up the water in the Jordan River. There's no water flowing into the "Salt Sea," also known as the "Dead Sea."

The Salt Sea is an amazing body of water. If you've ever swum in the ocean and swallowed some water, you know how salty it is. Well, imagine this. The Salt Sea, or Dead Sea, is about seven times as salty as the ocean. It's so salty that when swimmers jump in they can hardly sink. The salt holds them up! It's also called the "Dead Sea" because very few animals are able to live in it. The water is just too salty and stinky for much of anything to live.

Without Jesus in our lives we can get like that too. Our lives can become "stinky" without the freshness that Jesus brings. Give your heart to Him today and let Him freshen things up for you.

19 MARCH

Livin' off the Land

At that time the Lord said to Joshua,
"Make flint knives." Joshua 5:2.

When I was a boy I loved to read stories about Davy Crockett, Daniel Boone, and American Indians. I loved how they rode through the woods on their horses and took care of themselves. They made clothes out of animal skins, houses from trees, and tools out of stone. That's right, tools out of stone! I would love to have hiked across the land with them.

Some of those early American people, as well as the Israelites, would take a special stone called flint and make knives from it. Ancient people all over the world discovered that when they broke large chunks of flint, it would shatter into very long, very sharp pieces. It was just perfect for making knives. They also discovered that when they struck it against certain kinds of metal, it gave off a spark and was very good for starting campfires.

Did you know that God can use you to give off sparks too? He can use you to start the fire of God's love in someone else's life. Without Him we can also cut and hurt people, just like flint was used to cut things. Give your life to Jesus so you can be a sparker instead of a cutter.

It's Gorge-ous

It extended from Aroer on the rim of the Arnon Gorge, and from the town in the middle of the gorge, and included the whole plateau of Medeba as far as Dibon. Joshua 13:9.

The land of Canaan was called the "Promised Land." It was called that because God and Moses had promised a portion of the land to every person in Israel. As we read in Joshua 13:8, 9, some of the land given to three of the tribes had a gorge on it.

A gorge is a deep opening between walls of rock. These walls usually go straight down. If you were in the bottom of the gorge, you would have to look almost straight up to see the tops of the cliffs. The Royal Gorge in Colorado is more than 1,000 feet high at its highest point. A bridge has been built so you can drive from one cliff wall to the other. It's a scary sight looking straight down over the edge of the bridge.

Sometimes life gets scary too. It can be as scary as looking down over the edge of a cliff. But Jesus knows how to help us. If you'll just trust Him today and ask Him to help you, He'll get you over that scary time to the other side.

21 MARCH

Deeds on Steeds

Then thundered the horses' hoofs—galloping, galloping go his mighty steeds. Judges 5:22.

Now put your hiking boot in this left stirrup here. All right, now jump up and swing your leg over the horse and put your other foot in the right stirrup. All right, partner—you're ready to ride.

Now, that's exactly what I did, but that's not where I stayed. As I was galloping across the field, I noticed my saddle seemed to be slipping, slipping, slipping. Then I was riding under my horse. My saddle had slipped completely upside down. My head was hitting the ground. *Thud*—I fell off my upside-down saddle and onto the ground. Ouch!

That really happened to me. And that's what today's verse reminded me of. Our verse for today also describes a victory that Israel had because they obeyed God. That's a very important lesson. When I first read the verse, I thought the last part said, ". . . galloping go his mighty deeds." It made me think about the things we do for Jesus. When we serve Him through our actions, word gets around. Read Matthew 5:16. It tells us that people will see our good deeds and glorify Jesus. That's exactly what we want them to do. Do something nice for someone today. Your good deeds will go galloping on, and people will want to know more about the God you serve.

Miracle Coats

Look, I will place a wool fleece on the threshing floor. If there is dew only on the fleece and all the ground is dry, then I will know that you will save Israel by my hand. Judges 6:37.

Shhh. It's early morning, and we're hiking to the threshing floor. You see, God has asked Gideon to get an army together and fight the Midianites. Gideon really doesn't want to, so he's asked God for a miracle to prove that He'll stand behind Gideon. He's put fleece on the ground and wants God to settle dew from heaven on the fleece only. Look, God did it! He's amazing.

Fleece is made from the hair of a sheep or other animal. Weavers take the hairs, twist them together, and make thread or yarn to knit sweaters and coats. Some of the finest coats in the world are made of those little twisted sheep hairs.

Matthew 9:20, 21 tells the story of a sick woman who wanted to touch the edge of Jesus' coat. He didn't wear the finest coat in the world, so why did she want to touch it? She knew if she could just touch it, she would be healed. What great faith! Do you want Jesus that badly? I hope so. He really can make us into wonderful people if we'll just keep in touch with Him.

23
MARCH

Douse Those Coals

The men of Israel had arranged with the ambush that they should send up a great cloud of smoke from the city. Judges 20:38.

We've hiked right into a battle between the Israelites and the Benjamites. Look—the men of Israel are sending up a smoke signal so the rest of the army will know it's time to fight.

How did they make all that smoke? There's an old saying that goes "Where there's smoke there's fire." It means that even if you can't see the fire, if you see smoke, fire is under there somewhere just waiting to flare up.

You've probably seen the posters of Smokey Bear saying, "Only you can prevent forest fires." When camping, make sure your fire is completely out when you leave. Even if you can't see the fire burning, even if there's only smoke, it might still be there and start up again.

Anger can be like a smoldering fire. It can burn below the surface. If you hold it in too long, it can become a blazing fire. Don't hold it inside. Talk to Jesus about it and let Him know when you are angry. If you'll let Him, He can take it away and make sure it doesn't turn into a blazing forest fire that might burn you and the ones you love.

You Planted It

She went out and began to glean in the fields behind the harvesters. Ruth 2:3.

It's a good thing we have our hiking boots on today. We're in an Israelite's field gleaning, or harvesting, grain. We're pulling the kernels from the tops of the wheat plants. They can be ground up into flour and made into cakes and breads. Actually, grain is a word for the kernels of many different plants: wheat, corn, barley, and others.

The Israelite harvesters knew before they started harvesting exactly which type of grains they would be collecting. How did they know? Because they knew what had been planted in the field. You always get what you plant. If you plant corn, you get corn. If you plant wheat, you get wheat. If you plant barley, you get barley. If you plant righteousness, you get unfailing love. That's right. That's exactly what Hosea 10:12 says, and if God plants it, you get truth.

God wants us to reap love in our lives. He says we need to plant righteousness. We don't have any of our own, so that means we need to be with God all the time. Talk to Him in prayer, obey His Word, trust in Him to save you, and you'll glean exactly what you need—unfailing love. Now, that's a good harvest!

25 MARCH

Don't Be a Rat

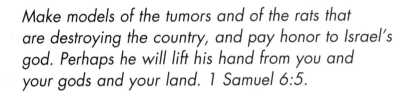

Make models of the tumors and of the rats that are destroying the country, and pay honor to Israel's god. Perhaps he will lift his hand from you and your gods and your land. 1 Samuel 6:5.

Models of rats. That sounds terrible. Who was making these models and why? The Philistines, enemies of the Israelites, had stolen the ark of the covenant. The Philistines had placed the ark in the temple of their own god, Dagon.

But now the Philistines were sending the ark back. Terrible things had happened. Their god had fallen over and was smashed, people were getting sick by the thousands, and rats were overrunning the land. The Philistines thought their only chance was to send the ark back with idols of the rats as a gift for the God of the Israelites. What a silly idea that was.

You know, even Christian people sometimes worship idols. It could be their car or their TV or their boat or their golf clubs. No, they don't bow down to them, but if those things take the time we should be spending with God, they become idols. All these things are fine as long as we don't forget to put God in first place. So forget the rats. Let's be models of the love of God.

Love Storm

Is it not wheat harvest now? I will call upon the Lord to send thunder and rain. And you will realize what an evil thing you did in the eyes of the Lord when you asked for a king. 1 Samuel 12:17.

Quit hiking and start running. Get under cover! Did you hear that thunder? It's dangerous out here. Do you like thunderstorms? As long as I'm safe, there's something exciting about them to me. The rain, the lightning, the crack of the thunder—God sure has created powerful forces in nature.

Thunder is an amazing sound. It's so loud! This is the way it happens. As lightning strikes, it heats all the air around it. Lightning is very hot, you know. The air heats so fast it explodes. That explosion is what thunder is. Whoa! Lightning really is hot.

Words can be like lightning and thunder. Sometimes words hurt and burn others. Sometimes they explode out of someone's mouth and hurt feelings, just like lightning, hurts when it strikes. When those powerful, hurtful words come out, they can sound as loud as thunder to the person they've hurt. Let your words be like a gentle rain. Let them water people's hearts and help love to grow. Create your own "love storm."

27 MARCH

Nice to Meet You, Cliff

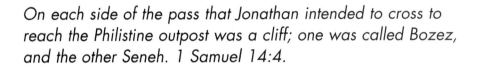

On each side of the pass that Jonathan intended to cross to reach the Philistine outpost was a cliff; one was called Bozez, and the other Seneh. 1 Samuel 14:4.

A cliff is a very high, steep rock wall. There was one on each side of the pass in this story. There was nowhere else to go. Jonathan and his armor bearer carefully hiked between these two cliffs toward the camp of the dreaded Philistines. Jonathan told his armor bearer if the Philistines said to come to them, they would know God would help them defeat their enemies. When the Philistines saw them, they said, "Come up to us and we'll teach you a lesson." When Jonathan heard those words he knew God would fight for them, and that's exactly what happened. You can read the whole story in 1 Samuel 14.

Sometimes things get tough. Maybe someone hasn't treated you very well. Maybe something you must do is very difficult. It may seem like there are high cliffs on either side of your life and nowhere safe you can go. Jesus always knows the way out of those difficult places. He can guide you safely through rocky cliffs and steep places. He will always help you through life's tight spots, and believe it—He will fight for you.

Hairy Numbers

"As surely as the Lord lives," he said, "not one hair of your son's head will fall to the ground." 2 Samuel 14:11.

Imagine you were very small. So small you could hike right through the hair on the top of someone's head. It would be like a great hairy forest. It would be so thick you couldn't even see—that is, if you weren't hiking on a bald head.

Can you guess how many hairs most people have on the top of their head? All right, did you think of a number? Here's the answer. Most people have between 100,000 and 150,000 hairs on the top of their head. That's so many!

Jesus said in Matthew 10:30 that God knows the number of the hairs on your head. Isn't that amazing? Jesus knows everything about us and He still loves us. Even though we make many mistakes, or say things we shouldn't, or do things that we're ashamed of, Jesus still loves us. He never stops. Whether we have hair on our head or not, I'm very glad God knows us so well and loves us so much.

Jumping Beans

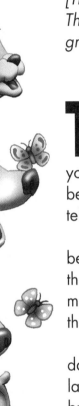

[They] brought bedding and bowls and articles of pottery. They also brought wheat and barley, flour and roasted grain, beans and lentils. 2 Samuel 17:28.

These men were very thoughtful. They hiked into the desert and brought all these things to David and his people. Did you notice that they brought beans? There are so many kinds of beans, and they're so good for you. Today, however, I want to tell you about a bean that really isn't a bean.

It's called a Mexican jumping bean. It's not really a bean, because it's the seed of a Mexican shrub. They jump because there are little caterpillars inside that will one day turn into moths and see the bright light of the sun. As they eat away at the inside of the seed, it makes the seed jump.

Sometimes the world we live in can be discouraging and dark. It can feel like we are trapped, just like the little caterpillar inside the bean. But one day soon we will also see a very bright light. It will come from the sky too. Jesus and His angels will burst through the clouds, and we who have been trapped in this dark world of sin will see the light of His coming and fly to heaven with Him.

Gray Wisdom

Deal with him according to your wisdom, but do not let his gray head go down to the grave in peace. 1 Kings 2:6.

Hike gently with those boots today. We're back on top of someone's head, someone's gray head. Actually, their head isn't gray; their hair is. Do you know anyone with gray hair? Do you know why hair turns gray? Here's the reason.

All through your life you have what is called pigment being pumped into your hairs. Pigment is what makes people's skin different colors. Pigment is color. When most people get older, the pigment or color doesn't get pumped into their hair as fast . . . and it turns gray.

Some people think that when a person gets older and their hair turns gray they aren't as useful anymore. It may be true that an older person can't move as quickly as they used to, or do some of the same things they could when they were young, but they have something young people do not have. They have experience and wisdom.

Remember, God has given us a great gift in the older, godly people around us. Ask them what they've learned from God in their many years and learn to be a better young person for Jesus.

31 MARCH

I Can See Clearly Now

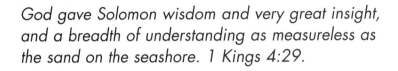

*God gave Solomon wisdom and very great insight,
and a breadth of understanding as measureless as
the sand on the seashore. 1 Kings 4:29.*

Wow! Solomon sure was wise. He had more wisdom than there is sand on the seashore. Now, I don't know exactly how much sand there is on the seashore. But I can tell you something really cool I learned about a special kind of sand called silica sand.

The sand you walk on at the beach is made up of millions of tiny bits of rocks. Silica sand, which is made mostly of quartz (a very pretty rock), is used to make glass. That's right. One of the ingredients of the glass in your windows is sand. Silica sand is heated to a very high temperature and then cooled very quickly. That's how glass is made.

Sometimes problems in life can be like sand. You can't see through sand, and sometimes we can't see how our problems will ever go away. But God can give us the wisdom to know what to do for life's problems. He can take a sandy situation and make it clear as glass. Ask God to give you a dose of His wisdom today so you can see your way clear to depend on Him.

Preserve Me

Give orders that cedars of Lebanon be cut for me. 1 Kings 5:6.

Hiking through the woods. I just love it, don't you? I especially love the smell of the evergreen trees. Evergreen trees are the ones with needles that stay green all year. You know, like a Christmas tree.

One type of evergreen tree is the cedar tree. Its very special wood has a red tinge, but that's not what makes it special. It's special because it's rot-resistant and bug-repelling. That means it just won't rot and go bad like most wood does, and bugs don't want to go near it. Because cedar wood has these special characteristics, people make cedar chests to keep special things they want to save. Bugs won't get into a cedar chest to eat your things, and your things won't rot, either. We say that cedar wood preserves things.

Just like cedar wood, God can preserve you. Psalm 119:40 says: "How I long for your precepts! Preserve my life in your righteousness." We need to accept Jesus' gift of righteousness and give our lives to Him. He can preserve us for His second coming and for heaven, where the bugs will never bother us and nothing will rot.

Fruit in the Bathtub

The inside of the temple was cedar, carved with gourds and open flowers. Everything was cedar; no stone was to be seen. 1 Kings 6:18.

Solomon was building a beautiful new temple for God. According to today's verse, there were flowers and gourds carved on the cedar walls of the Temple. Gourds are special kinds of plants that produce strange-looking fruit. Most of them aren't good for eating.

But today I want to tell you about a gourd you can eat and use in the bathtub, too! It's called the dishcloth gourd. This amazing gourd, also called a loofah, can be eaten when it's small and green. As the fruit gets larger it turns a brownish color and grows to be about one foot long. When you peel off the skin and take out the seeds, it becomes a "sponge" or "bathtub scrubber." That's right. The next time you're hiking to the store with your mom, ask her to show you a loofah sponge.

Psalm 51:2 finds David asking God to "wash away all my iniquity and cleanse me from my sin." God is the best scrubber in the universe. He not only provides a fruit to keep us clean on the outside; He provides forgiveness to keep us clean on the inside. Now, that's really clean.

You're My Everything

On the walls all around the temple, in both the inner and outer rooms, he carved cherubim, palm trees and open flowers. 1 Kings 6:29.

Well, we've hiked right back to the Temple today. What a beautiful place it is. Not only are there gourds carved on the wall, but angels, flowers, and palm trees. Don't you just love palm trees? They're so beautiful. I love their leaves, and I love coconut cream pie. That's right. Coconuts grow on one type of palm tree.

But that's not all palm trees are good for. Are you ready for this? Palm trees are good for shelter, food, wood for building, fuel for fires, fibers for clothing, starch for food, oil, wax, soap, sugar, brooms, hats, mats, vinegar, and fruit drinks. They live and grow all over the world in mainly warm climates, and people use them for all of these things. What would they do without the palm tree?

Just like the palm tree is everything to the people who use them, God is our everything. He's our Father, Protector, Guide, Conscience, Big Brother, Salvation, Healer, and many other things. He really is our everything. He wants to do so many things for you today. Ask Him into your heart and watch Him take care of everything.

4
APRIL

Standing Firm

The Lord will strike Israel, so that it will be like a reed swaying in the water. 1 Kings 14:15.

And just where have we hiked today? Careful, you might get your hiking boots wet. We're at the edge of a swamp, and just like today's verse says we can see reeds swaying in the water.

Reeds are large grasses that live on the edge of lakes and swamps. Some of them are very tall—up to 16 feet! There are reeds that live in the Far North and reeds that live in the warm breezes of tropical islands. One thing that all reeds have in common is swaying. They're so flexible that whenever the water moves, the reeds move with it.

It's good to be a flexible, cooperative person, but we must also stand firm and tall for Jesus. We need to stand up for those who are being mistreated—we need to stand up for the things that God teaches in His Word. Our verse for today tells us that Israel was about to be punished by God because they didn't stand up for Him. God doesn't want to punish—He wants to bless. Stand firm for Him—don't sway like reeds in the swamp.

Up, Up, and Away

As they were walking along and talking together, suddenly a chariot of fire and horses of fire appeared and separated the two of them, and Elijah went up to heaven in a whirlwind. 2 Kings 2:11.

Imagine that! Elijah raised right up to heaven in a whirlwind. He was riding in a chariot of fire. What a sight to see! Do you know what a whirlwind is? It's a sort of mini tornado. On windy days you might have seen dust and paper being picked off the ground and spinning round and round. The dust and paper gets carried higher and higher into the air. Elijah was carried higher and higher until he reached heaven. What a ride that was!

Sometimes the people we choose to be with can be like either whirlwinds or bathtub drains. Some people are happy, uplifting people with wonderful things to say. They're like whirlwinds carrying you up to bigger and better things. Some people are like bathtub drains. The words they use and the things they talk about can pull your spirits right down, just like a bathtub drain. Choose your close friends very carefully. Lift each other up with good thoughts and just you watch—others will want to get in on your whirlwind too.

6 APRIL

New Fig in Town

Then every one of you will eat from his own vine and fig tree and drink water from his own cistern. 2 Kings 18:31.

Look at these rows and rows of trees we're hiking through today. They're fig trees. If you'll read through the Bible, you'll notice that figs are mentioned many times. The fig is a deliciously sweet fruit that is very good for you. People in Bible times would put them in cloth bags and take them on trips because figs gave them energy for their journey.

When someone wanted to grow another fig tree they did it in a really cool way. When it was winter and the trees were sleeping, the farmer would cut off a branch and stick it in the ground. One year later that fig branch would have taken root in the ground and grown another three feet!

Sometimes things happen to us that make us feel like those fig tree branches. Maybe you have to move and are put in another town. Sometimes families split up and children feel alone. Even though those times can be very sad, Jesus can help us grow in our new place. Whenever you feel like the fig branch, remember that trusting in Jesus can help you grow into a strong person in a new place.

Hide and Seek

By your messengers you have heaped insults on the Lord. And you have said, "With my many chariots I have ascended the heights of the mountains, the utmost heights of Lebanon. I have cut down its tallest cedars, the choicest of its pines. I have reached its remotest parts, the finest of its forests." 2 Kings 19:23.

His name was Sennacherib. He said many evil things against God. In our verse today we see some of the terrible things that Sennacherib was saying. He was even proud that he had cut down Israel's finest forests. But the king was about to have a fall.

Why would the king think that cutting down Israel's forests was such an insult? It's because forests were very important to the Israelites. They provided shade from the heat of the day and wood for fires and building houses. They even made a really good place to hide if an enemy king was after them. That's why King Sennacherib was bragging about cutting down Israel's forests. Maybe he meant the Israelites couldn't even hide from him.

Just like a forest, God can hide and protect us. He can give us a home in His love. Ask Him to protect you today and be happy that Satan can never hurt you when you are in the forest of God's love.

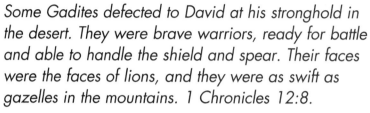

Just Out of Reach

Some Gadites defected to David at his stronghold in the desert. They were brave warriors, ready for battle and able to handle the shield and spear. Their faces were the faces of lions, and they were as swift as gazelles in the mountains. 1 Chronicles 12:8.

What brave warriors those soldiers in today's verse were. You would have had to keep those hiking boots moving pretty fast to keep up with them. The Bible says, "They were as swift as gazelles in the mountains."

Gazelles are small deerlike animals that run and turn very quickly. If you were fast enough to get close to one, it would quickly turn and be gone.

Sometimes wishes can be like gazelles. Sometimes we want things and just never seem to get them. In Philippians 4:12, 13 Paul said he had learned to be happy whether he had a lot of things or none at all. You may never have a lot of toys or other things, but that isn't what's really important in life.

Jesus is standing right in front of us today. He's not running away from us like the gazelle or those things we want so badly. He's standing with His arms wide open and inviting us to come to Him. Hike right into His arms today and discover the best treasure of all.

From Iron to Steel

He provided a large amount of iron to make nails for the doors of the gateways and for the fittings, and more bronze than could be weighed. 1 Chronicles 22:3.

Iron is such an amazing metal. If you've looked around while we've been hiking with God's people you have seen some. It's all over the earth. In fact, much of the earth is made of iron.

Iron can also be combined with many different things to make other useful materials. One of those materials is steel. When iron is combined with just the right things and heated to just the right temperature, steel is made. Steel is a very hard metal that cars and many other things are made of. Iron is pretty good stuff, but it can't beat steel for strength.

God has made us very special people, but like iron, we need something extra to make us the very best people we can be—we need God! We need Him to make good choices in life, we need Him to stand strong in difficult times, and without God you and I could never spend eternity in heaven with Him. Our lives will be so much stronger and happier with God. Let Him turn you into a steel-strong Christian in this weak old world.

10 APRIL

Who Threw the Moon Out?

They were to do the same . . . whenever burnt offerings were presented to the Lord on Sabbaths and at New Moon festivals and at appointed feasts. 1 Chronicles 23:30, 31.

We're on a night hike. It's beautiful. The air is fresh, the sky is clear, and the moon—wait a minute—where is the moon? I think I can see it—sort of. What's that? Our Israelite guide is telling us it's a new moon tonight. What's a new moon?

Way back on January 1 we talked about the moon reflecting the sun's light. As the moon moves around the earth sometimes it comes right between the sun and us. The sun is shining on the backside of the moon, and the side of the moon you can see is dark. When this happens it's called a new moon.

Some days seem like the dark side of the moon. We just can't see the light that usually cheers us up, but remember this: God's light and love are always shining. He's always taking care of us. Some days we may not be able to see it, but as the days pass by, just as we can see the moon again, we'll be able to see God's light again. There are dark times in life, but know that God's light will shine on you again.

Hard Work Tastes Good

He made interwoven chains and put them on top of the pillars. He also made a hundred pomegranates and attached them to the chains. 2 Chronicles. 3:16.

Today we've hiked right into Jerusalem and right up to the most beautiful building I've ever seen. It's Solomon's Temple. Solomon has decorated it so amazingly. He's even put chains on the tops of the pillars and hung pomegranates on those chains. M-m-m, pomegranates are so sweet and juicy.

Pomegranates grow on trees and have a tough, leathery skin on the outside. I like to cut them in half and pick out the little seeds. The pomegranate seeds are covered with a sweet, red, juicy pulp. I like to put the seeds in my mouth and chew the pulp off of the seeds. It's work, but they are delicious.

Many things in life take hard work too. You might want to be a teacher or a builder or a doctor. It will take you many years of hard work to be prepared to do those things well. But if you ask God to help you work hard at the things He wants you to do, one day you'll be just like a pomegranate seed. All that hard work will make for delicious things you can do for Jesus.

12 APRIL

Dead Skin—Dead to Sin

Nevertheless, you are not the one to build the temple, but your son, who is your own flesh and blood—he is the one who will build the temple for my Name. 2 Chronicles 6:9.

Flesh. Skin. What's it there for? Well, it's pretty waterproof. If you're out hiking like we are and get rained on, you don't get waterlogged. Just under your skin you have muscles and sensitive internal organs like your stomach and liver. Your skin is one of the things that help protect your insides.

So many things to learn about skin, but there's still more. Did you know the outside layer of your skin is actually dead? That's right; it's dead—and believe it or not, that's a good thing.

The Bible says in Romans 6:11: "In the same way, count yourselves dead to sin but alive to God in Christ Jesus." Just like the dead skin on the outside of you protects you from injury to your insides, believing that Jesus saves you from sin will protect you from sin and give you a new life in Him. Being dead is usually not a good thing, but dead skin and being dead to sin are exactly what you want.

Barely Smart or Barley Smart

Jotham made war on the king of the Ammonites and conquered them. That year the Ammonites paid him a hundred talents of silver, ten thousand cors of wheat and ten thousand cors of barley. 2 Chronicles 27:5.

The Ammonites paid Jotham 10,000 cors of barley. Do you know what barley is? Here's a clue. You could hike through a field of it, pick some heads, grind them up, and then bake bread. You see, barley is a grain like wheat or oats.

But guess what else is made from barley. Beer! That's right. The very same grain that's used to make nourishing bread is also used to make poisonous alcohol. Isn't it amazing that something so good can be used to make something that causes so much trouble?

You and I are a little like barley too. We can make good choices or bad choices. The same person can choose to do things God's way or choose to do them Satan's way. God will never force you to choose Him, but I can tell you this—God really does know what's best, and choosing His way is choosing the smart way. So don't be barely smart—be barley smart.

Not Just Ordinary Grass

Whatever is needed—young bulls, rams, male lambs for burnt offerings to the God of heaven, and wheat, salt, wine and oil, as requested by the priests in Jerusalem—must be given them daily without fail. Ezra 6:9.

Ezra 6:9 shows us that God wants everything from His people. Ezra tells us that one of the things God wanted the people to bring for an offering was wheat. Yesterday as we were hiking through a barley field we discovered the Israelites used it to make bread. Wheat is also another grain. Like barley, it can also be used to make bread.

Actually, both wheat and barley are types of grasses. Imagine that—making bread out of grass. We don't usually think of eating grass. We think of mowing it and putting it in bags and throwing it away, but God made special kinds of grass that grow seeds we can eat.

God also considers you to be very special. You're so special He sent His Son to die so you can be in heaven forever with Him someday. Today while we're hiking through this field of wheat, remember this: God loves you. You are special, and He's coming back for you someday.

God and You Make Bronze

The king, his advisers, his officials and all Israel present there had donated for the house of our God. I weighed out to them . . . 20 bowls of gold valued at 1,000 darics, and two fine articles of polished bronze, as precious as gold. Ezra 8:25-27.

Wow! The king, his officials, and the people of Israel sure donated a lot for the new Temple. Look at the last part of today's verse. They gave "two fine articles of polished bronze, as precious as gold." We're going to take a little hike to the bronzemaker's shop today to find out what bronze is.

It's hot in here. The bronzemaker is pouring that very hot liquid metal into another container of liquid metal. The larger container of metal is melted copper. The smaller amount of silvery colored metal is tin. But why mix the two together? Because when you pour a little bit of tin into the copper, it makes the copper much stronger. This mixture of the two metals is now called bronze.

God wants to pour Himself into your life just like the bronzemaker pours the tin into the copper. God knows if you'll let Him do that, you'll become a stronger person for Him. Ask Him to come into your heart and make you strong for Him today.

Beat the Sneak Attack!

Tobiah the Ammonite, who was at his side, said, "What they are building—if even a fox climbed up on it, he would break down their wall of stones!" Nehemiah 4:3.

Oops! Today it looks like we've hiked right into the middle of a mess. Cyrus, the king of Persia, told the Israelites they could go home after 70 years of captivity in Babylon.

Nebuchadnezzar had burned down the walls of Jerusalem many years before and now the prophet Nehemiah is encouraging the people to rebuild the walls. As they're building the walls, Tobiah and many more of Israel's enemies are making fun of them. Tobiah was trying, in a very sneaky way, to keep Israel from being able to protect themselves. Tobiah says, "If even a fox climbed up on it, he would break down their wall of stones!"

Foxes, those small relatives of the dog family, are thought to be very sneaky. Satan is too. In his very own sneaky way, Satan tries to get us too busy to build a friendship with Jesus. Don't let him do that. Make an appointment with Jesus each day and build a wall of protection that will keep that sneaky old fox out of your heart.

Stubborn as a Mule

There were 736 horses, 245 mules. Nehemiah 7:68.

Wow! Two hundred and forty-five mules is a lot of mules. Mules are usually known for two things. One is for being stubborn—the other is for being super hard workers. Mules can work longer, harder, and put up with more rough treatment than most other animals. They really are stubborn. They simply refuse to give up when their master tells them there's work to be done. That's a very good thing.

Maybe you and I should be a little more like mules sometimes. Old Satan tries to get us to give up on things too easily. It might be reading the Bible or praying or being kind to someone who hasn't been kind to us. He knows if we give up, no one will be happy. You and I won't be happy if we give up on doing good things. The people we do good things for won't be happy either, because they won't be receiving the blessings God wants to give them through us. Don't let Satan slow you down. Be "as stubborn as a mule" and never give up doing good things for other people.

18 APRIL

Fresh and Clean

"Go out into the hill country and bring back branches from olive and wild olive trees, and from myrtles, palms and shade trees, to make booths"—as it is written. Nehemiah 8:15.

The people of Israel were happy. They had finally returned from captivity in Babylon. As they read God's law, they discovered God had commanded them to observe a special feast called the Feast of Booths. They hiked out to the countryside to find branches from many different trees to build the booths. After they built them, the people lived in them for a few days celebrating the end of the fruit harvest.

A myrtle, one of the plants the people took the branches from, is an evergreen bush. Evergreen plants usually have some kind of needles that don't fall off when the weather gets cold. That's why they're called evergreens. Myrtles also smell good. It must have been nice to sit in those shady booths with the air smelling so fresh and clean.

Are you like a myrtle to the people around you? Do people enjoy being around you because you're cheerful and things just seem fresh and clean when you're around? I hope so. When people ask you why you're so nice, tell them that Jesus refreshes your life.

Beautiful Under Pressure

The garden had hangings of white and blue linen, fastened with cords of white linen and purple material to silver rings on marble pillars. There were couches of gold and silver on a mosaic pavement of porphyry, marble, mother-of-pearl, and other costly stones. Esther 1:6.

Today we've hiked right into the book of Esther as the king is showing off his wonderful palace. Today's verse says there were marble pillars in the palace.

Marble is a beautiful rock that's used in building fine buildings and carving beautiful statues. One very interesting thing about marble is that it wasn't always marble. Does that sound confusing? Here's what I mean.

One type of marble used to be another rock called limestone. Limestone is a grayish rock made of fossilized animals. When earthquakes and volcanoes put pressure and heat on the limestone, it can be changed from ugly old limestone to beautiful marble.

Have your parents or teachers ever punished you? It's not fun, is it? Remember this—just like heat and hard times can change limestone into marble, learning hard lessons can help change you into a better person. Remember, your parents and teachers are helping you learn important lessons in life. Let them help you, and each day you'll become a wiser, more beautiful person.

Beautiful on the Inside and the Outside

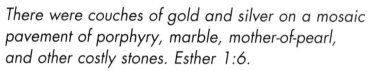

There were couches of gold and silver on a mosaic pavement of porphyry, marble, mother-of-pearl, and other costly stones. Esther 1:6.

Here we are again hiking through King Xerxes' palace. Look at all the beautiful things he used just to make the pavement around the palace. One of those things was mother-of pearl, and one of the places to get mother-of-pearl is from the abalone shell.

An abalone shell can be found in the ocean. From the outside it looks pretty ugly. But if you look on the inside you'll see the most beautiful thing. It's so smooth. When you move it around under the light, it seems to change colors. I can understand why Xerxes chose mother-of-pearl to be in his sidewalk.

Sometimes people can look a little like the outside of an abalone shell. Maybe their temper or a bad habit doesn't make them seem very nice on the outside. But like God, we should find out what's on the inside of a person's heart. As you do that, you'll find something worthwhile in everyone you meet. Who knows? God may be asking you to help that person learn more about Him and become more like mother-of-pearl on the outside, too.

Stronger Than the Strongest Wind

Suddenly a mighty wind swept in from the desert and struck the four corners of the house. It collapsed on them and they are dead, and I am the only one who has escaped to tell you! Job 1:19.

What a sad story we've hiked into today. A mighty wind from the desert came and blew down the house that Job's children were in. That sure must have been a strong wind.

Have you ever heard of a cyclone? A cyclone is a spiraling storm, like a tornado. It happens near the equator or the center part of the earth and has lots of water and wind spinning around.

Even though winds can be very dangerous and powerful, there is *Someone* more powerful than even the strongest wind. His name is Jesus. One night as a terrible storm was blowing, Jesus commanded the wind to stop and be still. Guess what? It did! The people around Jesus said, "Who is this? Even the wind and the waves obey him!" (Mark 4:41).

God truly is the king of the universe. He can control the strongest winds, and He can control your life, too. Give your life to Him today. He'll help you through the storms of life.

Wonderfully Made

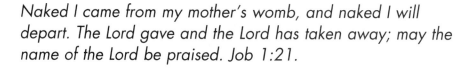

Naked I came from my mother's womb, and naked I will depart. The Lord gave and the Lord has taken away; may the name of the Lord be praised. Job 1:21.

Did you know you were alive before you were born? That's right. You lived in a warm, dark, safe place until you were ready to live in this world. Where was this warm, dark, safe place you lived? You might have heard people say you were in your mommy's tummy. Actually, you were very close to your mommy's tummy, but not *in* it. You were in your mommy's womb. It's the special place that God made for babies to grow before they are born.

One day thousands of years ago this earth was a little like your mother's womb. It was dark, but Someone was still there. It was God. And just like you came to see the light when you were born, God created light and made the earth full of life.

I'm so glad that God is our Creator. He created our world and all the wonderful things of nature. He also created you. He made you wonderful, too. You can thank Him for creating you by serving Him and filling other lives with His light.

Shining Star

May its morning stars become dark; may it wait for daylight in vain and not see the first rays of dawn. Job 3:9.

In case you hadn't noticed, we've hiked right into the book of Job. And we'll be here awhile because there's so much to learn in this wonderful nature-filled book.

Job 3:9 talks about morning stars. If you're up and awake just after the sun has risen in the morning, you may notice a very bright star. It's the last one to be seen as each bright new day begins. We call it the morning star, but it actually isn't a star at all. It's the planet Mercury. Mercury is never far from the sun, and it always seems to be reflecting the sun's light.

When we started our hike on January 1, we talked about the moon reflecting the sun's light and how we need to reflect God's love. Today we find out from the planet Mercury how to stay reflecting God's love. Just like Mercury stays close to the sun, we need to stay close to God. We need to think about Him, talk with Him, and tell others about Him. As you do this, you can't help reflecting God's love. Just like Mercury naturally reflects sunlight, you and I will begin reflecting Sonlight.

24 APRIL

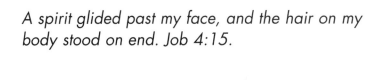

Runnin' Scared

A spirit glided past my face, and the hair on my body stood on end. Job 4:15.

On today's hike we're going to talk about being afraid. Have you ever been so scared that the hair on your arms stood on end? I have, and in today's verse it sounds as though Job was that scared.

Many things happen to your body when you're really scared. Your heart may pump faster, your skin may tingle, you may become stronger, and you may be able to run faster than you normally do.

Most of us don't like being afraid, but there are some things we *should* be afraid of. The Bible tells us we should flee from worshiping idols (1 Corinthians 10:14), run from evil desires (2 Timothy 2:22), and get away from the love of money (1 Timothy 6:10, 11).

You see, God does want us to be afraid of evil. He knows if we try to defeat Satan by ourselves we will fail. But don't be too afraid. When you run to the arms of Jesus you will be protected. When you're safe with Jesus, your heart's pounding will slow and the hair on your arms will lie back down again. Jesus is our great protector. Let Him take care of you today.

The Eyes Have It

A form stood before my eyes, and I heard a hushed voice. Job 4:16.

Eliphaz was a friend of Job's who said, "A form stood before my eyes." Now Eliphaz wasn't sure what the form was, but he did see it. He saw it the same way most people see things—with their eyes.

Eyes really are wonderful things. They are made of many different parts that all work together to help a person see. None of the things that are seen, however, would be understood unless your eyeballs were connected to your brain. That's right—your eye sees, but the optic nerve, the cord that connects your eyeballs to your brain, must send the message to your brain so you can figure out what you're looking at.

The Bible tells us in 1 Corinthians 2:14 we must have God's Spirit in order to understand the things of God. The Holy Spirit is like the optic nerve. You can read the Bible, but unless God's Spirit connects you with God, you won't really understand what God is saying. Ask for the Holy Spirit to open your eyes and help you understand God's Word right now.

26 APRIL

Speaking of the Tongue

You will be protected from the lash of the tongue, and need not fear when destruction comes. Job 5:21.

If you were very tiny and could climb (with your tiny hiking boots) right into someone's open mouth and stand right on their tongue, you would be amazed and probably a little bit frightened. You might be shaken up and down and thrown back and forth as the person was speaking.

What did Eliphaz, Job's friend, mean when he said that God would protect Job from the lash of the tongue? I think he meant that some people use their tongue to whip people. They speak words in a certain tone of voice that sound so mean and terrible. If you've ever been "whipped" by someone's tongue, you know how much it hurts.

God wants us to use our tongues to speak kind and loving words. Try this. Right now find someone near you and say something kind to them. Did you do it? Didn't it make you feel good? Didn't it make that person feel good? Our tongues can do so much harm when we use them to "whip" people. Use your tongue to speak words of love and see how the tongue can cause someone else to smile.

126

Poison Arrows Won't Hurt Me

The arrows of the Almighty are in me,
my spirit drinks in their poison. Job 6:4.

Wow! Poison arrows. That sounds scary. Did you know there really are poison arrows? It's true. The Indians of South and Central America use them to kill the birds and animals they eat for dinner. Do you know how they make the arrows poisonous? Here's the secret. There are frogs called arrow-poison frogs that live in the jungle and whose skin is moist with poisonous juices. The Indians rub their arrow on the frog's skin, and that's how their arrows become poisonous.

Satan has poisonous arrows too. The Bible says in Ephesians 6:16 that we should "take up the shield of faith, with which you can extinguish all the flaming arrows of the evil one." Our shield of faith will protect us against any arrow that Satan shoots at us. Having faith means we believe Jesus died for us, we believe He loves us, and we believe He saves us. So don't worry about Satan's arrows. When you and I believe in Jesus, our protector, we don't have to worry at all. The arrows will fall to the ground and never hurt us.

You Cream Puff

Is tasteless food eaten without salt, or is there flavor in the white of an egg? Job 6:6.

Are you ready to be hungry for dessert? Hike right into my kitchen. My wife is making the most delicious cream puffs. They are light and flaky balls of sweet dough filled with deliciously sweet whipped cream. M-m-m-m, are they good!

I asked my wife how she made them so light and fluffy. She told me the secret. Are you ready? It's the egg whites. That's right. When she's mixing up the dough she whips in some egg whites. When the cream puffs come out of the oven they're so light and flaky. I just can't stop talking about them. I just can't wait to get one in my mouth. Egg whites make all the difference. If it weren't for egg whites those cream puffs would be little clods of dough that no one would eat.

You can be like an egg white, you know. You can be the kind of person who brings sweetness and lightness to everything you do. With a smile and a good attitude, you just might cheer up the sourest person around. So when someone calls you a cream puff, tell them, "Thank you very much," and give them a great big smile.

Warm Smiles Melt Much Snow

When darkened by thawing ice and swollen with melting snow. Job 6:16.

I live in Colorado. During the winter huge amounts of snow fall and pile on the Rocky Mountains. The snowcapped mountains are beautiful as the sun shines down. It makes the snow look like it's covered with glitter. It makes for a gorgeous winter hike. But even though the snow is beautiful, it's very dangerous. Avalanches, getting lost in a blizzard, and freezing are things you don't want to mess with.

Even though most of the farmers who live in Colorado don't live in the mountains, they pray that lots of snow will fall on the mountains. They know that in the spring when the snow begins to melt, much of it will come to them and their crops as refreshing water.

You might have noticed that adults and even children sometimes have bad days. It seems their happiness is covered by cold snow that keeps them from smiling. Try this! Find someone who looks like they are having a bad day and give them the biggest smile you can. Just as the spring sun melts the cold snow on the mountains in Colorado, you too can melt the snow in someone's heart with a beautiful, warm smile.

Weak Webs

What he trusts in is fragile; what he relies on is a spider's web. Job 8:14.

Let's hike right up into my yard and onto my porch. Spiders love my front porch. They build beautiful webs that I knock down. I've found everything from grasshoppers to flies, to moths and butterflies, to other spiders caught in the webs of the spiders on my front porch. They sure do catch a lot of food in those webs.

But even though spiderwebs are great for catching small insects, there's one thing I've never found caught in a spider's web—a human being. No, I've just never seen a person caught in a spider's web, have you? Of course that would be silly. A person would be too heavy and too strong to be trapped in the web of a tiny spider.

As silly as that is, today's verse talks about a person who trusts in a spider's web or anything else in this life that is weak. What the writer meant is that we need to trust in strong things and not rely on weak things. The Bible calls God "our Rock." That means He's strong, He can be trusted, and He will never fall apart on us. Give your trust to God today and let Him be the rock of your life.

Help!

He shakes the earth from its place and makes its pillars tremble. Job 9:6.

Have you ever been in an earthquake? If you have, you know how scary it is. Earthquakes are caused when pieces of the top layer of the earth move and bump into each other. Things shake, fall down, and sometimes drop into large cracks in the ground. No one I know likes earthquakes, because they cause so much damage.

Rescue people are very important after earthquakes. One of their jobs is to look through all the broken-down buildings and knocked-over houses to look for people. Sometimes it takes days to find people who have gone without food and water and who have been injured badly. But the rescuers never give up. They continue looking day and night until they're sure everyone is safe.

God is a rescuer too. Did you know that? The Bible says in 2 Peter 3:9 that He doesn't want anyone to perish. That means He wants everyone to choose to go to heaven with Him. Call Jesus for help. Ask Him to rescue you from sin today. Choose to accept eternal life, and God will pull you out of sin's earthquake.

Testing, Testing, Testing

Does not the ear test words as the tongue tastes food? Job 12:11.

Quiet now. Try not to make a sound with your hiking boots. Today we're taking a hike to find aliens. Look, they're right over there—little green men with antennae. Unbelievable. Look, they're saying something to us in alien language. Wait, what's that? Oh, it's just their alien language translator. They use that so we can understand what they're saying. Listen. They're saying, "There's no such thing as little green men with antennae."

Did you believe that? Of course there are no such things as little green men from another planet with antennae sticking out. Remember this: "Don't believe everything you hear." That's what our verse for today is telling us. It's saying we should think about and decide if the things we hear are true. Some people think if you see something on television or read about it in a newspaper that it must be true. Beware—the things you read and hear aren't always true.

In Acts 17:11 Paul said the people of Berea were doing the right thing by checking their Bibles to see if what Paul said was true. The Bible is the book God has given us to test words by. Read it every day to see if the things you hear are true.

Powerful Flowers

He springs up like a flower and withers away; like a fleeting shadow, he does not endure. Job 14:2.

Today we're hiking down a sidewalk. What do you notice? Are there cracks? Do you see the seams concrete workers made in the cement every few feet? Wait—is that a flower? How did that flower grow up through the sidewalk? Look at that. It actually cracked the cement. That's amazing! A soft, beautiful flower can crack a sidewalk.

When we think of power, we often think of a bodybuilder working out in a weight room or a huge truck hauling dirt from a big hole in the ground. When we think of power, we don't usually think of a fragile flower. But just like that tiny flower can push its way through a hard sidewalk, God's love can find its way into the hardest heart.

Maybe you know someone who seems to have a hard heart. Sometimes it's because their feelings have been hurt and they don't trust anyone who tries to be nice to them. Keep showing them God's love. Never give up. Just like that flower can work its way through thick, hard cement, God's love can make its way into the heart of even the toughest person. Be one of God's powerful flowers today.

Give It Away and Back It Comes

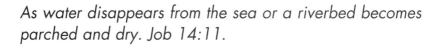

As water disappears from the sea or a riverbed becomes parched and dry. Job 14:11.

Today's verse is telling us that water disappears from the sea. Do you know where the water goes? Although you and I can't see it, it does go somewhere. It's what we call evaporation.

When the sun warms the water, the water turns into tiny little particles and rises into the sky. As the water gathers in the sky it forms clouds. When the clouds get heavy with water, it rains, and down the water comes back to the ocean. It makes a big circle; from the ocean to the sky and back to the ocean again.

The Christian life is like that. The more we give, the more we receive. God tells us He loves a cheerful giver and wants to bless us with all the things we need. Whether it's your time, your money, or anything else, don't be afraid to give it away when God asks you to. Read Malachi 3:10. You'll discover that if you give of yourself, like the ocean gives its water to the sky, God will give you more than you can imagine. Just keep giving—God will give back to you. It's His circle of love.

Skippin' Smooth

Water wears away stones and torrents wash away the soil. Job 14:19.

Have you ever been driving down a road with your parents and suddenly part of the road disappeared—or maybe the bridge was gone? Maybe as you've hiked in the woods you've seen that the side of a hill has been completely washed away. That's erosion.

Erosion is what wind and water can do to the earth. I love walking on the beach and picking up the smooth, round stones and skipping them along the top of a lake or ocean. Do you know how these stones got so smooth? Erosion. As the waves of the ocean come into the shore, slowly but surely they smooth the rough edges of the rocks. After many years, the sharpest, most jagged rock can become round and smooth.

In today's verse Job was talking about God's power and how He can wash anything away. It sounds scary, but actually it's a good thing. God can take the rough edges from our character and make us smooth and lovable. He can take the roughest, toughest person and make them kind and loving. Let Jesus come into your heart today. He'll make you smooth and easy to handle, just like the skipping stones on the beach.

Clean and Pure

His archers surround me. Without pity, he pierces my kidneys and spills my gall on the ground. Job 16:13.

I just love clean fresh water, don't you? It tastes so good when it's clear and clean. I have a special water pitcher in my refrigerator that cleans the water from my kitchen faucet. You see, the water in my house doesn't taste very good. But when I put it in my special pitcher, the water runs through a special filter. When it's done, it tastes so delicious.

Did you know you have special filters in your body? You do! They're called kidneys. They take poisons out of your blood. Most adults have five quarts of blood in the tubes that carry blood around their body. Kidneys clean one quart every nine minutes. They really are fast and powerful filters.

Satan is trying to poison our world with sin. But Jesus doesn't want us to be poisoned by sin. If you and I will study God's Word each day—if we'll stick close to Jesus all the time—He has the power to keep us clean and pure, just as your kidneys keep your blood clean and pure. Stay close to Him and let Him filter out the sin in your life.

Venomous Words

*He will suck the poison of serpents;
the fangs of an adder will kill him. Job 20:16.*

Whoa! Now, that's a scary verse. Maybe you've seen a poisonous snake at a zoo or on a television program. I hope you never see one on a nature hike. While most poisonous snakes won't hurt you if you don't bother them, they can be very dangerous. Never go near one.

Most poisonous snakes have long fangs or teeth coming down from their upper jaw. These fangs are actually hollow tubes that carry venom or poison. When a poisonous snake bites an animal it's going to eat, it injects its venom into the victim and kills it. It sounds very sad, doesn't it?

Unfortunately, that's the way nature works in a sinful world. Sometimes people can be like poisonous snakes. I don't mean they have fangs, but the words that come from their mouths can be like poison. Words can hurt a person's heart very badly. They can be just as painful, in a different way, as a poisonous snake's bite.

Choose to let Jesus take control of the words that come from your mouth. Let Him make your words as sweet as honey. Use your words to make people feel good and lead them to their heavenly Father.

Bones and Blood

His body well nourished, his bones rich with marrow. Job 21:24.

All right, now stand up. Are you growing tall? Do you know what keeps you standing straight and tall? It's your bones. Yes, there are other parts of your body that help you stand up, but it's your bones that grow longer, which makes you stand taller and helps you hike longer.

In today's verse Job says that bones are rich with marrow. Did you think that your bones were just bone, all the way through? They're not. Your bones are filled with soft Jell-O-like stuff in the middle. This substance is called marrow, and it's very important. You see, all the blood cells in your body are made there. Different kinds of blood cells carry oxygen to all your muscles, provide you with energy to run and play, and protect you from being sick all the time. Your blood cells and your bone marrow work together in a very important way.

Isn't God wonderful? Now you understand how He made your bones and your blood to work together. He wants us to work together with each other, too. He wants us to cooperate so others can see what His love can do. People will know when we work together with others that God's love changes hearts.

Flying High With Jesus

How then can a man be righteous before God? How can one born of woman be pure? If even the moon is not bright and the stars are not pure in his eyes, how much less man, who is but a maggot—a son of man, who is only a worm! Job 25:4-6.

On today's hike we've discovered something that's just plain yucky. It's a dead animal. Oooh, there are little white worms eating the animal. These little white worms are called maggots and will one day turn into flies. Yuck. Why would God talk about maggots in His Word? It must be important for some reason. Let's see if we can find out.

In today's verses Job is saying that no one is good enough to be righteous before God. That means you and I cannot go to heaven without God's help. Job says we are like maggots—worms! It's true that God created us all special, but Job is saying we need to depend on Him completely to be saved. We can live forever with Jesus only if we accept His forgiveness and His death on the cross.

You, of course, are much more special than a yucky old maggot, but always remember: Only with Jesus will you and I "fly" to heaven.

Changes in You

The house he builds is like a moth's cocoon, like a hut made by a watchman. Job 27:18.

Look through your binoculars! Do you see that fuzzy little brown sack? It's a cocoon. Inside that cocoon a caterpillar is changing into a moth. It was a green caterpillar. When it breaks out it will be a pale-green luna moth. Luna moths are very large, very beautiful, very pale-green moths that fly around at night. How could that chubby little caterpillar have changed into the beautiful and graceful luna moth? Only by a miracle of God—that's how.

God can change you, too. He can take the things that aren't so perfect in your life and change you into the person He wants you to become. But just like the caterpillar went all by itself into its cocoon, you too must spend time alone with God.

Try this. Take a blank notebook and when you pray, write down things you want to say to God. Each day add more to your book. This will help you stay in touch with God, and just like the clumsy caterpillar turns into the graceful luna moth, you too will turn into a graceful Christian who will lead others to Jesus.

Shining Like Gold

The earth, from which food comes, is transformed below as by fire; sapphires come from its rocks, and its dust contains nuggets of gold. Job 28:5, 6.

On today's hike we're rock collecting. We're looking for a precious gemstone that Job called sapphire. Rock collectors today believe that what Job called sapphire in his time is called lapis lazuli today.

Lapis lazuli is a beautiful rock with a deep-blue color. People polish it up and make jewelry because it's so beautiful. But it's not beautiful just because it's such an amazing blue. It usually has little pieces of pyrite in it. Pyrite is also known as fool's gold. It is called fool's gold because many people have been fooled into thinking it was gold. Imagine how amazing lapis lazuli must be—deep blue, with little pieces of gold-colored pyrite. Some people think it looks like the deep-blue night sky with shining stars.

God can shine in you even brighter than pyrite shines in lapis lazuli. He wants to put His character in you. He wants people to notice there's something special about you. What's special is God's love. Be like lapis lazuli today. Shine like the stars so you and others can fly to the stars on your way to heaven someday.

Hiding in Him

Coral and jasper are not worthy of mention; the price of wisdom is beyond rubies. Job 28:18.

Today as we hike along the shore, I want you to look out into the ocean. Can you see that area of the water that looks very shallow? It looks shallow because there are many coral skeletons rising up from the bottom of the sea. All those coral skeletons together form a coral reef.

But let's back up. What is coral? Coral is an animal without a backbone that grows on the ocean floor. When the coral dies, its skeleton becomes very hard with minerals in the water. The coral skeletons look like plants growing from the bottom of the sea. But here's the really cool thing about coral skeletons. They're great hiding places. All kinds of beautiful fish and amazing sea creatures live in the coral reefs.

God is an even better hiding place than a coral reef. The Bible says in Psalm 32:7: "You are my hiding place; you will protect me from trouble and surround me with songs of deliverance." Isn't it wonderful to know God has provided a place for the creatures of the sea to hide, and that He's given us a place to hide in Him too?

142

The Touchstone

*Coral and jasper are not worthy of mention;
the price of wisdom is beyond rubies. Job 28:18.*

Here we are, hiking right through Job 28:18 again. That's because this verse has so much of God's nature in it. Today we're rock collecting again, and we've found jasper. It's a very special type of jasper called black jasper. It's so special because it can tell when gold is around. Here's how it works.

If you found a piece of rock that you thought might have gold in it, you'd want to know for sure, wouldn't you? But how could you tell? That's where black jasper comes in. Just rub your gold rock on a piece of black jasper. If the streak that was left on the jasper was a certain shade of yellow, you'd know you had gold. Easy as that!

When black jasper is used in this way it's called a touchstone. A touchstone tells you if you've got the real thing. The Bible is a touchstone, too. You can tell if someone's words and life are true (or not) by testing them with the Bible. I'm so thankful God has given us a touchstone. Check out your life and words with the Bible today. See if God is changing you into the real thing.

Mr. Mohs

The topaz of Cush cannot compare with it; it cannot be bought with pure gold. Job 28:19.

I don't know about you, but I love these rock-collecting hikes. God did such an amazing thing when He made so many different colored rocks and minerals.

Wait, look at that. It's beautiful! That very pretty stone is called topaz. Topaz comes in many colors, but today we've found clear topaz. Do you want to know a secret? If you cut topaz just right it looks exactly like a diamond. That's right. You'd never be able to tell the difference if you didn't know about Mohs' scale of hardness.

One of the ways you can identify rocks that look exactly alike is by knowing which rock is harder. You see, on Mohs' scale of hardness, diamonds are the hardest. If you scratched a piece of topaz against a diamond, the topaz would be left with a scratch and the diamond wouldn't. That's because the topaz is softer than the diamond.

Sometimes people can leave their scratches on you too. But even though others may not treat you well, decide to be like Jesus and return good for bad. Who knows? God may be able to soften that hard person up when their scratches bring out love and kindness in you.

Dew Be, Dew Be, Dew

My roots will reach to the water, and the dew will lie all night on my branches. Job 29:19.

Hiking in the very early morning can get your feet all wet. Even if it hasn't rained, dew can make the ground wet. Dew is formed at night when the earth becomes cooler than the air. The air around us contains tiny drops of water too small to see. When the earth is cooler than the air, those tiny drops gather together into larger drops on the ground. And that's how dew is made.

Do you remember the story of Gideon? God wanted to use Gideon to defeat Israel's enemies. Gideon didn't understand why God would want him, so he asked God for a sign. One night Gideon put the wool of a sheep on the ground. He asked God to keep it dry and let the dew fall all around it. The next night He asked God to make the wool wet while the ground around it stayed dry. And God did both!

Our God is a God of miracles. If He can make the dew fall where He wants it, He can make a miracle in your life, too. Do you need a miracle today? Don't be afraid to ask. He loves to help!

16 MAY

Putting On My Armor

Let my arm fall from the shoulder, let it be broken off at the joint. Job 31:22.

Ouch! That would hurt. Why would Job want his arm to fall off? I'll tell you why. Job wanted to be so close to God that he would rather have his body fall apart than sin against Him. Wow, Job must have loved God very much.

Today's verse talks about the shoulder. Do you know what your shoulder is good for? One thing it does is to help you move your arm all around. Your shoulder can also help you carry heavy loads.

Your shoulder also helps you to play games. When I take off my hiking boots and put on my hockey skates to play hockey, I wear all kinds of equipment. For example, I wear shoulder pads so it won't hurt when I bang my shoulder on the ice.

Just like I put on my hockey "armor" to protect me from getting hurt, Ephesians 6 tells us we need to put on God's armor to protect us from being hurt by Satan. Read Ephesians 6 and find out what the armor is. When you find out what it is, put it on. God's armor is the only safe way to protect us from our enemy, the devil, and will keep us as close to God as our friend Job was.

Smooth as Ice

Who gives birth to the frost . . . when the waters become hard as stone, when the surface of the deep is frozen? Job 38:29, 30.

When does water become hard as stone? When it's ice, of course. Today let's take off our hiking boots and put on ice skates. That's it, slip your feet in; now lace them up; now carefully stand up. There, you're standing on the ice in your skates. Now push off. Look at that—you're gliding across the ice.

Have you ever noticed that ice gets more slippery if there's water on it? It's true—when you slide across ice with water on it, you go faster. Actually, that's what happens when you skate. When the blade on your skate slides on the ice it actually rubs that little bit of ice and melts it. You skate smoothly and quickly because you're actually skating on a layer of water.

God's Holy Spirit has melting power too. Sometimes people's hearts can be cold. Maybe they've been hurt by others and their heart is as hard as ice. But the Holy Spirit can glide across an icy heart and melt it.

The Holy Spirit can use you to do the same thing. Do you know someone with a frozen heart? Ask God's Holy Spirit to fill your life with kindness and melt away some ice today.

Jumping Over Problems

Do you know when the mountain goats give birth? Do you watch when the doe bears her fawn? Job 39:1.

I love to drive into the Rocky Mountains. They're so big and beautiful and full of nature. One of the animals I love to see is the mountain goat. Mountain goats look like big furry goats with long white beards. Most adult mountain goats can jump as far as 11 or 12 feet. See how far you can jump. Go ahead and try it. Did you jump as far as the mountain goat?

It's an awesome sight to see mountain goats jump from one rock to another, missing deep holes and dangerous cliffs. They seem to know just how far and how high to jump to stay out of danger.

God has given us the stories of many people in the Bible. These stories include all the good things and bad things these people did. God gave us these stories as examples so we wouldn't make some of the same mistakes they did. You and I will make mistakes in our lives but, just like the mountain goat leaps over dangerous areas in the mountains, God wants us to avoid as many of life's problems as possible. Read God's Word today and, like the goat, jump right over the problems God has warned us about.

Flap Your Wings for Joy

The wings of the ostrich flap joyfully, but they cannot compare with the pinions and feathers of the stork. Job 39:13.

Get those hiking boots ready to move. If one of those ostriches starts chasing you, you'll want to run as fast as you can. Ostriches can run up to 40 miles per hour. Maybe God gave them so much speed because they can't fly. That's right, ostriches are birds that can't fly.

But our verse for today says the ostrich flaps its wings joyfully. Why would an ostrich be happy when it flaps its wings but never gets off the ground? Well, maybe the ostrich is happy because it's always with friends. Ostriches live in groups of five to 50. Or maybe it's happy because it can run so fast. Really, I doubt the ostrich is happy for either of those reasons. I'm sure it's happy just being an ostrich. That's what God made it to be.

Sometimes you and I might be unhappy with who we are. Maybe we don't like something about the way we look. Or maybe we're frustrated because we can't run as fast as one of our friends. Remember, God made you the way He did for a very important reason. So flap your "wings" joyfully and thank God for making you so special.

20
MAY

Flying Gracefully

The wings of the ostrich flap joyfully, but they cannot compare with the pinions and feathers of the stork. Job 39:13.

Wow! We're still hiking through Job 39:13. Today we see another big bird—it's the stork. Some kinds of storks can stand more than five feet tall. That's a big bird. From today's verse we see that the stork, unlike the ostrich, can fly. It flies so gracefully with its neck stretched out in front and its feet trailing behind it.

Flying gracefully. It's like living gracefully. Do you know what living gracefully means? It means giving of yourself. Jesus has given us His grace, His gift of salvation. He came to this earth. He healed people. He helped them, and He taught them about His Father in heaven.

God wants us to give to others, too. He wants us to give of our time, our money, and ourselves to help those around us make it gracefully through each day. Most of all, God wants us to give Him to those around us. By the life we live and the words we say, He wants us to tell our friends and family about Him. He wants us to tell them so that one day we can all be winging our way gracefully through the sky and on our way to a heavenly home.

Big Teeth, Little Problems

Look at the behemoth, which I made along with you and which feeds on grass like an ox. Job 40:15.

Careful, now—we're hiking into strange territory today. Look, it's a behemoth! What's a behemoth? you say. Well, Bible experts don't know for sure, but some think it might have been the hippopotamus. What God was saying to Job was "I made the hippopotamus, I made you, and I can certainly take care of your problems."

Would you like to know why making a hippopotamus was such an amazing thing? Well, hike right down by the river today, and we'll take a look at the mighty "hippo." Look at those teeth. They're huge. Some of the lower teeth can grow more than 12 inches above the gumlines. Think of how hard it would be to chew if your lower teeth were that long. It's true—God did an amazing thing when He made the hippo.

But just as God told Job He would take care of his problems, we can trust God to take care of our problems, too. After all, if God can make a beast 15 feet long with 12-inch teeth, I know He can make a way for us when we have problems too big for us to fix.

22 MAY

Rise Above It All

Can you pull in the leviathan with a fishhook or tie down his tongue with a rope? Job 41:1.

All right, animal hunter—today we're hiking through the swamp. Easy now, what's that? Look closely. That, mate, is a crocodile. We think what Job called the leviathan in today's verse is what we call a crocodile today.

What an amazing animal the crocodile is! They can grow 20 feet long and weigh more than 1,500 pounds. They're fast, too. For a short distance they can run as fast as a horse. But they don't usually run to catch their food; they swim. If you've ever seen a crocodile in a pond in the wild or on a television program, you've noticed they just float in the water with only their eyes sticking above the surface. They can see what's coming into the pond from above the water while their body is completely covered by water.

In a way you and I should be like the crocodile. Sometimes we get buried in problems the way the crocodile gets buried in the water. But with eyes of faith we can look over our problems and know that God will take care of us. So use your "eyes of faith" today and "rise above it, mon."

Rotting Wood Is No Mistake

Iron he treats like straw and bronze like rotten wood. Job 41:27.

Today we're hiking through the woods. I just love the woods—the smells, the animals, the flowers, the rotten trees. Rotten trees—now, why would anyone like rotten trees? They're really not pretty, they can't grow any leaves, and sometimes they even smell funny. Well, here's the reason I like rotten trees.

Some insects call rotten trees home. That's right! Many insects live off the rotten insides of dead trees. That means many little insects grow up to be big insects and become food for the beautiful birds I love to watch in the woods.

Another reason I like rotten trees is that they feed the soil. They become food for all kinds of plants, including beautiful flowers and many other new trees.

If trees could think, they might believe when they're rotting that they've failed. After all, they're not standing tall sprouting leaves anymore. But rotten trees do all kinds of good things, don't they?

When you make a mistake and fail at something, what do you do? Do you get angry? Do you get frustrated? Even when you make mistakes, remember this—out of what seems like failure today can grow the most beautiful flower. Don't give up. God will help you grow through mistakes.

24 MAY

Whistle While You Work

You have granted him the desire of his heart and have not withheld the request of his lips. Selah. Psalm 21:2.

Have you ever thought about how amazing your lips are? You use them to test how hot your hot chocolate is. You use them to kiss your mommy and daddy good night. You can wrap them around a straw to drink a drink. You can even pucker them up, blow air through them, and whistle.

I always thought whistling was the coolest thing. You can whistle a high note or a low note. You can change all the notes at the right time and whistle a song. Isn't that amazing? You can whistle a song that someone else can sing along with. If you whistle a song about Jesus' love or His care for you, you could even cheer yourself up if you're not feeling too well.

When Paul wrote the letter to the Philippians he was in prison. Even though he could have complained and everyone would have understood, he chose to be joyful. Read Philippians and see how many times Paul mentions the word *joy*.

Choose to be joyful today. No matter how you're feeling, choose to be thankful and whistle a tune. You might just cheer up everyone around you in the process.

Bacteria Busters

Who may stand in his holy place? He who has clean hands and a pure heart, who does not lift up his soul to an idol or swear by what is false. Psalm 24:3, 4.

Can you guess what most moms say to their children when they hike into the house after playing outside? Wait, don't guess yet. What do most moms tell their children to do before they come to the supper table? You guessed it. They tell them to wash their hands.

Do you know why moms want their children to wash their hands? Bacteria. Bacteria are very small animals that can be seen only with a microscope. Certain kinds of bacteria can cause you to catch a cold. They live everywhere, and you can kill many of them by washing your hands with soap and warm water.

Today's verse talks about clean hands and a pure heart. Of course, God wants us to wash our hands, but in this verse He's talking about something different. In this verse, clean hands and a pure heart means that God wants us to keep our hearts and our hands away from evil. He knows what harm sin can do.

When you wash your hands today, remember that God wants all of you to be clean—inside and out. Wash your hands with soap and keep your heart pure by sticking close to Jesus.

26 MAY

Mr. Brainy

*Test me, O Lord, and try me, examine
my heart and my mind. Psalm 26:2.*

Today we're hiking again. Do you know what part of your body makes you able to hike? If you said your feet or your legs, you're only partly right. Of course, there are many parts of your body that help you hike, but the one I want to talk about today is your brain. Did you know your brain helps you hike? It does. In fact, your brain helps you do everything you do.

If the ground is heading uphill, your brain tells your feet and helps them make the next step correctly so you won't fall. If you need to jump across a stream while you're hiking, your brain helps your feet know how hard and how far to jump.

Your brain is amazing, but it can also cause you to do bad things. The Bible says that our minds don't want to follow God. We need to be close to Him so His Holy Spirit can control our thoughts and help us do the right thing. Let's ask God to examine our mind, as David did in today's verse. He'll help us think thoughts that will help us live for Jesus.

Be Strong

My life is consumed by anguish and my years by groaning; my strength fails because of my affliction, and my bones grow weak. Psalm 31:10.

Oh, that sounds painful! Today's verse talks about bones growing weak. Think how hard it would be to hike with weak bones. You and I sure would get tired more quickly.

Some people suffer from a disease called osteoporosis. When bones don't get all the vitamins, minerals, and exercise they need, they grow weak. They can become so weak and brittle they can break without much trouble.

Sometimes people can become weak and brittle too. Sometimes they can even break. I'm not talking about people's body; I'm talking about people's courage. Courage is something that makes us strong when we need to stand up for what we believe. True courage comes only from God.

How can you and I make sure we stand up for the right and don't become weak and brittle? Just like bones need the right food and exercise to stay healthy, we need to eat "food" from God's Word and exercise our prayer "muscles." Stay close to Jesus, and He will give you courage to do the right thing and keep you from breaking like weak bones.

What a Mighty God We Serve

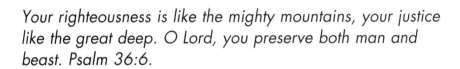

Your righteousness is like the mighty mountains, your justice like the great deep. O Lord, you preserve both man and beast. Psalm 36:6.

I was in Colorado on a visit when I was 14 years old and decided that someday I would live there. When I was older I did move to Colorado, and I've lived here now for 12 years. Why do you think I love Colorado so much? If you look closely at today's verse, I think you'll be able to guess why. Did you guess? I love Colorado because of the mighty mountains. I've stood on the tops of some of them, and the view is beautiful. They're so beautiful when they're all snowy white with fluffy clouds hanging around their tops.

Today's verse says that God's righteousness is like the mighty mountains. God is the perfect king of the universe, and that's why His righteousness is mighty. God performs miracles, and that's why His righteousness is mighty. God's love is perfect, and that's why His righteousness is mighty.

I'm so glad that we have a mighty God. A God whose love and righteousness are perfect, and a God who will give that love and righteousness to you and me so that we can become more like Him. What a mighty God we serve.

Oh, My Aching Back

My back is filled with searing pain;
there is no health in my body. Psalm 38:7.

Ouch, ouch, ouch! My aching back. Slow down there, hiker. My back hurts. It seems like David's back was hurting him too. He said his back was "filled with searing pain."

Do you know someone who has a bad back? Sore backs can be caused by many different things, such as a bed that's too soft or too hard, lifting heavy things the wrong way, or even by standing wrong. That's right, standing up the wrong way can give you a very sore back.

We call the way we stand "posture." It's important to stand up straight and tall. Not only does it make it easier for you to breathe, but it keeps all the muscles in your back in the right place. If you and I slouch for too long, we can make our backs sore.

Standing tall and true for Jesus can keep us from trouble. In the Bible God has told us to stay away from Satan and sin. He knows if we get too close to sin it will make us "slouch" and become hurt and sad. Stand tall and true for Jesus today so you won't have to complain about your "aching back."

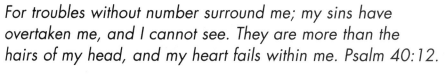

Heart Attack

For troubles without number surround me; my sins have overtaken me, and I cannot see. They are more than the hairs of my head, and my heart fails within me. Psalm 40:12.

Today we're going to talk about something very sad. Do you know what a heart attack is? When a heart is diseased or overworked, a person's heart can fail. Some people can even die from a heart attack. That's very sad.

It's important to keep your heart healthy. Your heart pumps blood all through your body. One of the ways you can keep your heart healthy is to get plenty of good exercise. Another way you can keep your heart healthy is never to smoke cigarettes or drink alcohol.

In today's verse David says his heart is failing because his sins have overtaken him. He feels guilty and dirty with sin. He probably isn't having a heart attack, but his sins are making him feel so bad that his heart is hurting.

Do you know what the answer to David's problem is? Forgiveness. God's forgiveness can make us clean and keep our heart from hurting. We still need to make things right with the people we've sinned against, but isn't it good to know God will forgive us completely? Now, that makes my heart feel much better.

Are You Thirsty?

As the deer pants for streams of water, so my soul pants for you, O God. Psalm 42:1.

All right, hiker. Step quietly. It's getting dark out here in the woods. Look all around you. If we're lucky, we might see a deer tonight. Quietly now. Shh. Look over there. Isn't she beautiful? She's a doe with her baby fawn. Uh-oh, she saw us. Wow, look at them run! They jump so high. I know that mama and her baby will be very tired and thirsty when they get done running so far and fast.

Today's verse talks about a deer that pants for a drink of water—a thirsty deer that has run a long way. What did God want us to learn from today's verse? Well, it's right in the second part of the verse. God wants us to thirst after Him like a deer that has run all the way across a huge field.

God wants us to learn to love Him so much that we need and want Him just as badly as the food we eat and the water we drink. In fact, God wants us to know we need Him even more than we need water. Take a deep drink of Jesus' love today and never be thirsty again.

1 JUNE

Crashed, but Not Burning

Deep calls to deep in the roar of your waterfalls; all your waves and breakers have swept over me. Psalm 42:7.

We're almost there now. Do you hear the roar? Now, look over the edge. Wow, that's a long way down. It's 3,212 feet down to be exact. And it's so loud! Do you know where we are? We're at Angel Falls in the country of Venezuela in South America. Angel Falls are the tallest falls in the world.

You might be wondering why they're called Angel Falls. You might think it's because they look heavenly or because they're so tall the angels might be at the top. Well, it isn't anything quite that amazing. It's because a man named James Angel, an American explorer, crashed his airplane nearby and discovered them many years ago. What a discovery—and all because James crashed his plane.

Sometimes the best discoveries in life are made when we crash—when we make mistakes. We may think we've failed because we've made a mess of things, but that's exactly when God wants to teach us how important it is to depend on Him.

So the next time you make a mistake, thank God that He's about to teach you something important. You might make one of the greatest discoveries of your life.

Tough, but Sweet

*All your robes are fragrant with
myrrh and aloes and cassia. Psalm 45:8.*

On today's hike we're looking for a special plant called the cassia plant. Look, there's one. I know it doesn't look so special—in fact, it looks like many other plants. But we want the cassia plant for its bark. Watch this. We'll peel off the bark like this and set it in the sun to dry. Once it's dry we'll grind it up. Once it's ground up we'll put it in our food. Why—because ground-up cassia bark tastes like cinnamon.

Many people are like the cassia plant. They seem a little tough on the outside, just like the bark of the cassia plant. But on the inside they really are sweet people. So you might wonder why they act so tough. Sometimes it's because someone has hurt their feelings. They don't want that to happen again, so they don't let anyone get to know them.

You might be just the person God wants to use to soften that person up and show them how wonderful God's love is. Be God's servant today and peel that toughness off the people around you. Let them know about the sweetness God wants to put into their life.

3
JUNE

Always

A psalm of Asaph. The Mighty One, God, the Lord, speaks and summons the earth from the rising of the sun to the place where it sets. Psalm 50:1.

It's very early today. In fact, it's so early it's still dark. Listen to the *crunch, crunch* of our boots. Wait, what's that sliver of light? Look, it's so beautiful. The sun is rising. The clouds are turning pinkish-orange. I just love to watch the sunrise and sunset. God's world is so beautiful!

Did you know that the sun doesn't really rise and set? It stays right where it is and the earth moves around it. That's what makes the sun look like it's moving. One thing's for sure—you can always count on seeing the sun each day. It's always there—so steady. It's that way because God made it that way, and we can always count on what He makes to stay in place.

Just like the sun is always there, God is always there too. He'll always answer our prayers, He'll always take care of us, and He'll always love us. I'm so glad we can always count on God to be there for us. Let's show Him how much we love Him by being there for those around us and showing them God's love today.

Melting Away

Like a slug melting away as it moves along, . . .
may they not see the sun. Psalm 58:8.

Slugs are small, squishy, wormlike animals that live in dark, wet places like gardens. They hide under rocks and plant leaves. The reason they like wet places is that they're made of mostly water. If they get too hot, the water starts leaving their body and they can die. Today's verse tells us about this. When it says the slug melts away, it means the sun is taking away the water in its body.

Watching a slug slowly melt away sounds like a sad story. What this verse is really talking about, though, is men who do not want to love God. Slowly but surely as they move further and further away from God, they melt away into sin. The harsh heat of Satan's world takes the life and love right out of them.

God wants you to live in the sunlight of His love. He wants to bless you so much. Best of all, He wants to give you all His love for free. Don't be like a slug and move away from God. Run to Him today, and let God fill you with life eternal.

"Long Live the King!"

5 JUNE

Increase the days of the king's life, his years for many generations. Psalm 61:6.

Long live the king, long live the king!" Many years ago, and maybe in some places still today, people would say this whenever the king was around. It was like saying, "You're doing a good job, and we want you to live for a long time and keep doing it."

Did you know there are things you can do to live longer? It's true—God has told us all about them in His Word. He wants us to live long, healthy, happy lives, and He told us just how to do it.

When God created Adam and Eve, He gave them a garden to take care of. It had plenty of fruits and vegetables and lots of fresh water. He wanted them to eat healthfully. He knew they would be much happier when the food they ate and the clear water they drank helped them feel their best. Remember, too, that He gave them a garden to work in. That included lots of exercise and hiking around that beautiful place. Open the Bible today and get your spiritual exercise. Remember, God is the king of the universe, and He wants you to live forever.

Give Your Brain a Drink

O God, you are my God, earnestly I seek you; my soul thirsts for you, my body longs for you, in a dry and weary land where there is no water. Psalm 63:1.

Are you thirsty? Go ahead—get a drink of water. Your body needs lots of water every day. Doctors say you should drink about eight glasses each day. Do you know why you need it so badly?

Every part of your body needs water. Your muscles need water to work hard when you play or work around your house. Your intestines need water to help clean them out. Even your brain needs water so you can think clearly and do well on your schoolwork.

Your brain controls everything you do. Scientists believe that when certain brain cells are in need of water, they tell you and cause you to walk to the drinking fountain and get a drink.

Because we have a sinful nature, our brain doesn't always tell us when we need more of God. We need to make a habit of praying and reading the Bible so we won't want to do without Him for even a day. Be thirsty for God, just as David was in today's verse. Drink of God's water, and you'll never be thirsty for Satan's things again.

7

Just a Little Patch of Grass

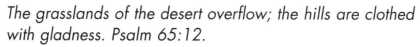

The grasslands of the desert overflow; the hills are clothed with gladness. Psalm 65:12.

Today we're hiking in the desert, just as the Israelites did thousands of years ago. Imagine having to hike for 40 years in a desert. That's what they did.

Some people think there's nothing in the desert but sand. There is a lot of sand for sure, but there's so much more. Let's hike over to that patch of desert grass. If you walk slowly and look carefully, you may see some residents of the desert grasslands. That's right. There are little creatures that live among the grass in the desert. Insects, scorpions, lizards, snakes, and others live in the grass because they know there's moisture and shade from the burning desert sun. All those creatures make the best of the little grass they can find.

Sometimes it may seem like you don't have very much. Maybe your friend has a toy you don't have. God wants us to count our blessings and be thankful for whatever He's given us. Be like the creatures of the desert that make the best of the little they can find. Be a thankful Christian who knows that even though you may not have a lot now, someday you'll live with a King who owns the whole universe.

As Cruel as Vinegar

*They put gall in my food and gave
me vinegar for my thirst. Psalm 69:21.*

Oh, yuck. Can you imagine drinking vinegar? I think it
would pucker my lips and make my teeth feel funny.
Today's verse explains what happened to Jesus when He was
crucified. The Bible tells us that when He was thirsty, instead of
water they gave Him vinegar. It seems they wanted to be as cruel
as they could to Him. What a sad, sad way they treated Jesus.

Have you ever been mistreated? It's so sad, but it happens
every day in many places all over the world. People make fun
of people; they treat each other very badly, they sometimes
even hurt and kill others.

How can we stop all this meanness? Here's the answer—
we can be nice to others. I've tried it, and do you know what
I've discovered? I've found when I treat others with kindness,
they usually treat me that way too. Imagine that. If you and I
started being really nice to people, and those people started
being really nice to other people because we were really nice
to them . . . well, just imagine what could happen. Don't be like
vinegar to a thirsty person. Today let's be like fresh, clean water
in a mean, thirsty world.

Run for Your Lives!

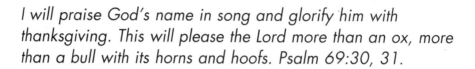

I will praise God's name in song and glorify him with thanksgiving. This will please the Lord more than an ox, more than a bull with its horns and hoofs. Psalm 69:30, 31.

Get ready to move those hiking boots today. We've joined a large crowd of people in the country of Spain. They do the craziest thing here. I'm not sure why, but here's what they do. Hundreds of people gather in the narrow streets of the town and let bulls with very sharp horns chase them down the road.

Why would people do such a crazy thing? Well, maybe some do it because it's exciting and maybe others do it because they believe someone will think they're brave. There are probably some who don't know why they do it.

Back in Bible times people brought sacrifices to God. Some were bulls with horns. God had asked them to do it. But sometimes they forgot that the reason they brought sacrifices to God was to show Him how much they loved Him.

Our verse for today says God wants us to sing to Him with a thankful heart. He wants to know we really love Him. Show Him today that you love Him with all your heart, and let Him know you haven't forgotten why.

Pain in the Neck

To the arrogant I say, "Boast no more," and to the wicked, "Do not lift up your horns. Do not lift your horns against heaven; do not speak with outstretched neck." Psalm 75:4, 5.

My neck was so sore. So I went to the doctor. He took an X-ray of my neck and discovered that one of the bones in my neck was pinching a nerve. I had stretched it the wrong way, and it was giving me pain.

Today's verse talks about another kind of person who stretches their neck the wrong way. Have you ever seen someone shouting at somebody else and telling them they know more than that other person? I have, and I noticed that the person boasting often sticks their neck out and tries to scare the other person. It really doesn't look very nice.

God doesn't want us to stick out our neck and boast. He's asked us to be humble. When we stick out our neck at other people, we're really sticking it out at Him. We're really saying that our way is better than His.

Be humble today. Pull your neck in and show people you love them. Love them as Jesus did when He was here on earth, and keep your neck from being a pain.

Rest in Peace

*Valiant men lie plundered, they sleep their last sleep;
not one of the warriors can lift his hands. Psalm 76:5.*

I really like to sleep. It feels so good to snuggle in bed under my warm goose down comforter and fall asleep on a cold winter's night.

If we went without sleep, bad things would happen. We wouldn't be able to think clearly. Our bodies would get sick. We wouldn't be able to see straight after many hours without sleep, and our friends wouldn't want to be around grumps like us.

Yes, sleep is a very good thing. God created us to need rest. When you sleep, your body grows. When you sleep, your body repairs itself. When you sleep, your brain is refreshed for another day of schoolwork and studying God's Word. Yes, sleep is very important.

There's another kind of rest that's also very important. You and I need to rest in God's strength. As we hike through the mountains in today's verse we see that God is very powerful. We can trust in Him because He loves us too. So don't worry about what will happen to you. As you fall asleep tonight, know that God takes care of you while you rest and that His strength protects you from every danger.

Muscle Man

With your mighty arm you redeemed your people, the descendants of Jacob and Joseph. Selah. Psalm 77:15.

Sometimes I hike to a nearby health club to "work out." I bring my gym bag with my tennis shoes, my workout shorts, and my T-shirt. After I get changed in the locker room I head to the room with the weights. I have a list of exercises I go through. I pick up those weights and start to strengthen my arms, legs, and stomach muscles.

Sometimes while I'm at the health club, really big muscular men come to work out. They pick up much heavier weights than I do and their muscles bulge when they lift. Sometimes I'm even embarrassed to pick up my little weights when the guy next to me is barely straining with weights four times heavier than mine.

Today's verse tells us about another person with mighty strong arms. It's God. It tells us that God is very strong and uses His strength to save His people. And we don't have to be embarrassed that God is stronger than we are; in fact, we can be thankful and happy that God uses His "mighty arm" to save us. Aren't you glad we have a God with big biceps on our side? I sure am!

13 JUNE

Clear and Sunny

He destroyed their vines with hail and their sycamore-figs with sleet. Psalm 78:47.

Button up that coat. Lace on those boots. It's going to be a cold hike today. In fact, it's sleeting! Have you ever seen sleet? Sleet is small drops of frozen rain. When it hits you in the face, it hurts. Like our verse for today says, it can even destroy trees and plants. When it lands on the leaves and branches it makes them very heavy. If they get heavy enough, they can break and destroy the plant.

Your words could be like rain. Words can be sweet and helpful and pleasant sounding. They can do others so much good. They can encourage and help and uplift. But words can also be like sleet. They can be hurtful. They can discourage, and they can destroy. They can make friendships turn very cold.

Ask Jesus to help you keep your words warm and friendly. Use your words to help and encourage others. Don't let them turn cold and hurtful like sleet. Good words are like good weather—they help us and others feel happy and pleasant. Keep the weather around your words clear and sunny, and brighten someone's day.

Problems Into Roses

Make them like tumbleweed, O my God,
like chaff before the wind. Psalm 83:13.

Today we're hiking in the land of the Bible. Wait—what was that blowing across the road in front of us? Look, it's a little tumbleweed. Actually, it's the seedpod of a plant called the rose of Jericho. The rose of Jericho is an amazing plant. When the weather is dry, the branches turn inward and protect the seedpod from getting too hot. When it rains, the branches turn outward and release the seedpod. When the wind blows, the little seedpod bounces across the ground spreading seeds for new rose of Jericho plants.

Sometimes when people have problems, they close up and keep to themselves. But God wants us to open up to Him just like the rose of Jericho opens up and lets its seedpod blow down the road. And just like the rose of Jericho's seedpod begins new life, God can take our problems and give our faith new life. He does that by showing us how He can solve them.

Open up to God today. Tell Him your problems. Let Him know you want Him to turn your problems into opportunities. Then watch Him perform miracles in your life and blow your problems down the road.

Prickles Into Velvet

I am like a desert owl, like an owl among the ruins. Psalm 102:6.

Wow, is it hot here! We're hiking in the desert today. It's starting to get dark—

Did you hear that whirring sound? Look over there—it's diving toward the ground. It's got something in its mouth now. Amazing—it caught a mouse in the dark. Look, it's flying again. Stop, owl! You're going to run into the—

It flew right into that cactus. No, I don't mean it ran into the cactus. It flew right *inside* the cactus. If you read today's verse, you know I'm talking about the desert owl. Many desert owls live right inside a cactus. It keeps them warm in the winter and cool in the summer. What's even better is that the owl didn't have to carve its home out of the tree. A woodpecker looking for insects did it for the owl. Imagine being inside of something so sticky and prickly. Ouch!

Sometimes people are sticky and prickly. Some people do things to hurt others on purpose. Jesus wants you and me to get right inside their hearts by being kind. Fly right into the hearts of prickly people on the wings of kindness. Let God use you to make a prickly person as smooth as velvet.

Better Than a Bird

The trees of the Lord are well watered, the cedars of Lebanon that he planted. There the birds make their nests; the stork has its home in the pine trees. Psalm 104:16, 17.

Today let's hike through the park near my house. We're going to look at leafless trees. In Colorado where I live, the leaves fall off the trees in October and November. Some people think the trees don't look as nice without their leaves. That may be true, but you and I can see something we can't see very well during the summer when the leaves are thick and green. Do you know what I'm talking about? That's right. I'm talking about bird's nests.

Our verse today tells us that God made the trees so birds would have places to build their nests. When He created this world, He was even thinking about where the little birds would live. That was thoughtful.

As much as God must love the birds, you are so much more valuable to Him. He loves you so much, and He's interested in all the little things in your life. He wants to hear the good and the bad. He wants to hear you tell Him all about your day. Why don't you kneel down right now and tell Him all about it?

17 JUNE

Just the Way He Likes Them

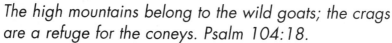

The high mountains belong to the wild goats; the crags are a refuge for the coneys. Psalm 104:18.

Today we're hiking in the mountains. Our verse tells us that living in the mountains of the Bible lands were wild goats and animals called coneys. What are coneys? The coneys of the Bible go by another name today. They're called hyraxes. A hyrax is an animal that looks a little like a rabbit, but has a plump head, short neck, ears, and tail; short, slender legs; a squatty body; and hooves on its back feet. That sounds like a funny-looking animal, doesn't it? That may be, but God made the hyrax just the way He wanted it to be.

While it's OK to say an animal is funny-looking, we should never talk about people that way. It's true that people come in all shapes and sizes, but it hurts their feelings if we talk about a person's shape or size being funny or strange or weird.

We are all very special to God. So special that He made us all different. So special that He wants us to treat each other with love and respect. So look for the beautiful things in all the people around you and love them because God made them just the way He wants them.

Roarin' for Dinner

The lions roar for their prey and seek their food from God. The sun rises, and they steal away; they return and lie down in their dens. Psalm 104:21, 22.

Careful now. Hike quietly. You just never know when we might come face to face with a lion. Hopefully we'll hear it roaring before we stumble around a corner and end up at its feet. Ouch!

Did you notice what today's verse says about the lion? It says they "seek their food from God." As big and powerful as lions are, they need someone else to provide dinner for them. They need God! That's an important lesson for us to learn too.

Sometimes people are tempted to think they don't need God. It's truly sad when people don't realize how much God has given them. I think God must be sad when we don't thank Him for His gifts to us.

Why don't you get down on your knees right now and thank God for giving you everything He's given you? Then try this—see if you can find someone to share your blessings with. It's a wonderful thing to roar about!

19
JUNE

Bruised Hearts

He sent a man before them—Joseph, sold as a slave. They bruised his feet with shackles, his neck was put in irons. Psalm 105:17, 18.

You want to talk about a long and difficult hike? Joseph was chained up and then traveled hundreds of miles across deserts to Egypt—sold as a slave. Our verse for today says the metal shackles put on his feet left bruises.

Have you ever had a bruise? Don't they hurt? Bruises happen this way: Something hits you, or maybe it's you hitting something else—like the ground. Ouch! Your skin turns red. It turns red because you've broken tiny blood vessels, and now you're bleeding under your skin. After a few days your bruise may turn black and blue or yellow and green. Dried blood turns colors.

Has your face ever turned red without even being hit? Mine has. My face turns red when I'm embarrassed. Embarrassing others can hurt them even more than a bruise. Many times that hurt doesn't go away after a few days. Sometimes it can stay for years or maybe even the rest their lives.

Jesus taught us to love each other, not to hurt and embarrass each other. Be the kind of person that heals bruised hearts and shows all of God's children what true love really is.

Just Nosin' Around

Their idols are silver and gold, made by the hands of men. They have mouths, but cannot speak, eyes, but they cannot see; they have ears, but cannot hear, noses, but they cannot smell. Psalm 115:4-6.

Today let's hike right into the kitchen. I want you to imagine that someone is cooking your favorite food. Maybe it's lasagna, or macaroni and cheese, or maybe it's chocolate cake. Doesn't it smell good? M-m-m, delicious! Now I want you to imagine your nose couldn't smell your favorite food. Why, that would take the fun right out of it, wouldn't it? Your nose is a wonderful thing. It warns you when there's a fire. It leads you to dinner. It even tells you when you've cooked dinner too long.

Today's verse is talking about the idols that people worship. It says they have noses, but they can't smell. As a matter of fact, they can't smell, taste, touch, see, or hear. Idols are pretty useless. You may not know anyone who bows down to an actual idol, but did you know anything that becomes more important to us than God is an idol? Give your all to God today. He's the one who gave you your nose, and He's the only one who can save you from sin.

21 JUNE

Stop Monkeyin' Around

May you be blessed by the Lord, the Maker of heaven and earth. Psalm 115:15.

If we could do it, I'd like us to take a quick hike around the world today. We'd see some amazing things. We'd see great mountains and volcanoes, giant birds and colorful lizards, beautiful rocks, funny-looking mammals, and so much more. God is such an amazing and wonderful Creator. He must be very smart to think of all the different things He created.

Did you know that not everyone believes God is the Creator of our world? In fact, some people don't even believe God is real. Some people think we came from monkeys. They believe that because monkeys can walk and do some of the things humans do, we must have been monkeys who changed into people. I guess if you don't believe there's a God, then people from monkeys makes sense.

What makes sense to me is that an all-powerful God created our world. We have the Bible, His Word. We see His miracles around us every day. And I know that only God could have made our bodies as wonderful as they are. Yes, there's no question for me. Monkeys are cute and funny, but God made you and me from scratch.

Be Satisfied

Drink water from your own cistern, running water from your own well. Proverbs 5:15.

When most people in the United States want a glass of water, they go to the kitchen, turn on the faucet, and fill up their glass. But not everyone has it so easy. In many small villages in other parts of the world, people have cisterns next to their house. A cistern is a large bathtub-like container that fills up with rainwater. When the people want some water to wash or cook or drink they take a bucket to the cistern and scoop out some water. They must be careful, though. They can't take all the water. Others in the house need it, and they never know when it will rain next. And it would be a very bad thing to steal water from a neighbor's cistern.

Today's verse says we should drink water from our own cistern. It doesn't mean we shouldn't share; it means we shouldn't covet what our neighbor has. It could mean that if our neighbor has a nicer car than we do, we shouldn't worry about it. Don't fret. God will take care of you. You might not get everything you want, but God will give you everything you need, and He'll make sure there's always enough living water for you.

23 JUNE

One at a Time

Go to the ant, you sluggard; consider its ways and be wise! Proverbs 6:6.

Be careful now. Do you see those big piles of sand? Look closely. They're moving. Well, they look like they're moving. Actually, they're anthills, and the reason they look like they're moving is that ants are constantly moving in and out of their anthill. They are such hard workers.

If you've ever stepped on an anthill, you've seen the ants immediately get busy rebuilding their home. The ants are so tiny and their homes are so big! How do they do it? Here's how—one grain of sand at a time.

Now look closely at today's verse. Do you know what a sluggard is? It's a lazy person. God doesn't want us to be lazy. We might wonder how we will ever get our room cleaned or the yard raked. You get it done the same way I've written these words for you—one shoe and one leaf at a time.

So don't be lazy. God has given you talents. He wants you to learn to use them by working hard. It starts by doing the little things like cleaning your room and taking out the trash. Look at the ants. They work hard. God says to learn from them—one at a time!

Cinnamon Friends

. . . myrrh, aloes and cinnamon. Proverbs 7:17.

M-m-m . . . it smells so good. Where are we today? We've hiked right into the bakery, and the baker is baking beautiful cinnamon rolls. Try to say that five times fast. They smell so good, and they taste even better. You can unroll them and see the dark, sweet cinnamon inside.

Cinnamon has been a favorite spice in many parts of the world for many years. In fact, at one time it was more valuable than gold. That's right. People wanted it that badly. Those ancient people used it for baking, but they had other reasons for using it, too. In Egypt it was used to preserve people's bodies when they died. It was used in perfume in other places and some even used it in medicine.

Do you know where cinnamon comes from? It comes from a special evergreen bush. The inside layer of bark is dried and ground up to make cinnamon.

Did you know you can be a cinnamon friend? It's true. You can be a friend who is more precious than gold. If you're kind and loving and honest to those around you, people will want a sweet person like you around. So get out there and spread a little cinnamon around today.

25 JUNE

Are You Green Today?

Whoever trusts in his riches will fall, but the righteous will thrive like a green leaf. Proverbs 11:28

Let's hike right up to this tree. Now look straight up. It's so tall. Look at all the green leaves. Did you ever wonder how those leaves turned green and stayed healthy? Do you know where their food comes from? Well, everything they need—the chlorophyll that turns them green, the water that keeps them healthy, the food that keeps them strong—comes from the ground. Next question. How do all those things get from the ground to the leaf? Roots, of course. The food and water travel right into the roots, right up the trunk, right out the branches, and right into the leaves. Isn't that amazing?

Do you know how to grow into a strong and healthy Christian? Roots, of course. Not quite like tree roots, but almost. Each day we need to talk with God in prayer and read His words in the Bible. When we do that God will give us all the spiritual food we need to be strong and healthy followers of Jesus.

Open God's Word today. Plant your roots deep in Him. Soak up the water of His salvation, and you too will grow tall in Jesus.

Lovin' Your Veggies

Better a meal of vegetables where there is love than a fattened calf with hatred. Proverbs 15:17.

Today we're hiking right down Mr. Farmer's very straight rows of vegetables. What's your favorite vegetable? Is it okra or spinach or kale? Could it be corn or carrots or brussels sprouts? Maybe it's green beans or turnips or lettuce.

In Bible times it seems that poor people ate more vegetables than rich people. That's because a poor person could grow their own vegetables and might not have enough money to own an animal they could eat for dinner. If a poor person had a cow or a goat they would use it to work or give milk. Only people with money could own enough animals to have some for dinner.

Now you can understand why Solomon said what he did in today's verse. He meant it would be better to be poor and have love in your family than to be rich and hate your family. Family love is very precious and important. It's in our family we learn to love and be kind to people outside our family. When you sit down to eat your next meal together, look at your corn or carrots or whatever vegetable you're having and remember to love your family.

27 JUNE

Happy Like a Rainstorm

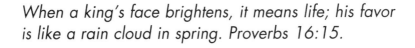

When a king's face brightens, it means life; his favor is like a rain cloud in spring. Proverbs 16:15.

I hope you waterproofed your hiking boots today. It's going to rain. Did you ever wonder how raindrops came out of clouds and how they got in there in the first place? Here's the story.

Old Mr. Sun, way up there in the sky, is very warm. He's so warm he can make little droplets of water float into the sky from rivers, ponds, lakes, oceans, and the puddle in your backyard. Pretty soon all those little droplets of water get together and make bigger droplets way up in the sky and form clouds. The droplets get bigger and bigger, until they're way too heavy to stay in the sky; then they fall to the ground as rain.

Today's verse says that "when a king's face brightens," he does so many good things—it's like rain pouring down from the sky. It sounds like a good idea to make the king happy, doesn't it?

It isn't much different today. If people are happy, good things happen. Try this. Make as many people happy as you can today. See if good things start to happen. I think you'll find when you make other people happy, you'll be happier too!

188

Blood Alert

Who has woe? Who has sorrow? Who has strife? Who has complaints? Who has needless bruises? Who has bloodshot eyes? Those who linger over wine, who go to sample bowls of mixed wine. Proverbs 23:29, 30.

Have you ever fallen while you were hiking? I have. I've skinned my knees and cut my arms, and the blood flowed. Do you know why even little cuts seem to bleed so much? Your brain sends instructions for your blood vessels to open wide and let the blood flow faster. The more blood that flows, the more white blood cells rush to the spot that needs fixing. Isn't that amazing?

Have you ever seen someone with bloodshot eyes? It seems like all the little blood vessels are opening wide to let lots of blood flow into the eyeball. It can happen when you get something in your eye like smoke or dust, but it also happens when people drink alcohol, as today's verse talks about.

That should tell us how important it is to keep our bodies free from poisons like alcohol. It does so many hurtful things. Just read today's verse again, and you'll see what I mean. Our bodies and God's Word can teach us so many lessons. The one they're teaching us today is to stay away from alcohol.

Watch Out, She's Gonna Blow!

*Like one who takes away a garment on a cold day,
or like vinegar poured on soda, is one who sings
songs to a heavy heart. Proverbs 25:20.*

Now, I know we've already talked about vinegar, but this is something a little different. This is vinegar on soda. Let me tell you about a fun thing I did one day when I was a boy.

I took some baking soda and poured it into a plastic bottle. Here's where the vinegar comes in. I took my plastic bottle and hiked outside because I didn't want to make a mess in the house. I slowly poured the vinegar into the bottle with the baking soda. Then I heard a bubbling noise, and mountains of foam shot out of the bottle. Wow, I had made a volcano!

Today's verse tells us when people are sad it sometimes hurts them to be around people who are happy. Laughing and singing while someone is sad is sort of like pouring vinegar on soda. It might make them angry. They just might blow. If they need someone to hurt with them, then be a good friend and hurt with them. See what they need and do what you can for them. That's what Jesus did!

Flying Curses

*Like a fluttering sparrow or a darting swallow, an
undeserved curse does not come to rest. Proverbs 26:2.*

Today our hike takes us into a cave. Do you hear that fluttering sound? I think it's coming from up above. I think they're bats. They're darting all over the place. Wait a minute. Those aren't bats. They're birds. They looked like bats from a distance, but now I can tell they're swallows. And look! Way up on the side of the cave are their little nests, attached with glue they made themselves.

Maybe you've seen swallows flying around your neighborhood. They dart and weave as they catch the insects they eat. One thing's for sure. They never seem to slow down. They never really seem to land anywhere.

Have you ever had someone say something about you that wasn't very nice? If that hasn't happened to you, it probably will someday. Today's verse says that "an undeserved curse does not come to rest." Like swallows, undeserved curses and bad words won't fall on you. When you've been nice to people, you have nothing to worry about. Others will know you don't deserve the bad things that are being said about you, and will respect you for always being nice. So don't worry about the "flying curses." They won't land on you.

1
JULY

Don't Be a Leech

The leech has two daughters. "Give! Give!" they cry. There are three things that are never satisfied, four that never say, "Enough!" Proverbs 30:15.

I was hiking in the woods one day when I heard the familiar sound of running water. *This is great,* I thought. I love to explore water. I might find some fish or water bugs or crayfish. When I found the water I was excited. "I'm going in," I said to myself. After an hour or so of exploring, I decided it was time to get home. I headed out of the pond and sat down on the bank to put my socks and boots back on.

Then I saw it. At first I saw only the blood running down the side of my leg. When I looked to see where it was coming from I was disgusted. Hanging off my leg was a big worm called a leech, and it was sucking my blood. Yuck.

The Bible says that some people are like leeches. They suck people dry. They're takers. They never seem to want to give to others. God wants us to be givers, not takers. Follow God's advice. A leech doesn't get much respect; a giver is loved by all.

192

Warm or Cold

There are three things that are too amazing for me, four that I do not understand: the way of an eagle in the sky, the way of a snake on a rock, the way of a ship on the high seas, and the way of a man with a maiden. Proverbs 30:18, 19.

Today those hiking boots are very important. Today you'll need protection. Protection from what? you say. Protection from biting snakes.

In today's verse Solomon says he just didn't understand the way of a snake on a rock. Maybe Solomon didn't know that snakes are cold-blooded animals and need to lie in the sun to heat their bodies up. Cold-blooded animals' bodies adjust to the temperature of wherever they happen to be at the moment. You and I are warm-blooded. Our bodies stay the same temperature no matter what the weather is.

Just as our temperature stays the same, we ought to be the same kind of people wherever we are. If you want to be a good example for Jesus, you need to be a good example all the time, no matter where you are and whom you're with. Don't be like the snake, which changes temperature wherever it happens to be. Be a warm-blooded Christian and live for Jesus all the time.

HWJ-7

3 JULY

The Noisiest Bird

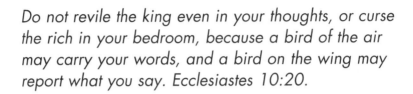

Do not revile the king even in your thoughts, or curse the rich in your bedroom, because a bird of the air may carry your words, and a bird on the wing may report what you say. Ecclesiastes 10:20.

Imagine hiking on a peaceful summer day. The sky is blue. The breeze is blowing gently. Suddenly the air is filled with the squawking and screeching of a blue jay. There's no doubt that the blue jay is one of the prettier birds around, but it's all spoiled when it opens its noisy mouth. You can hear it all over the neighborhood.

Did you know some people are like blue jays? They interrupt other people's conversations; they have to know everybody's business and then they squawk it all over town or school or church. They are called gossips. Gossiping hurts people. It makes them feel bad and turns people against each other.

Pray for those who hurt others by gossiping, and pray for yourself. Pray that you won't be a blue jay by sticking your nose in other people's business and shouting it all over town. Gossiping hurts. Don't do it yourself, and help others to stop.

194

A Rose Among Thorns

I am a rose of Sharon, a lily of the valleys. Song of Solomon 2:1.

Wow, what a great day! The sun is shining, and the air is warm. We're on a beautiful hike in God's creation. Look at that little bush over there. Can you see it? It's called a rose of Sharon bush. The flowers are so big and beautiful.

In today's verse Solomon called himself a rose of Sharon and a lily of the valley. Some people think this special poem was actually talking about Jesus. I like that idea. Jesus is like a very special flower. He brightens our day and makes everything seem beautiful.

I think that's the way Jesus wants you and me to be. I think He wants us to brighten people's day. I think He wants us to make everything around us beautiful. Can you think of a way you might be able to do that? Hey, if you and I keep a smile on our faces and look for ways to cheer others up, we could be like a rose in our world. Let's try it today, OK? With Jesus shining through you, people will notice His love and want to be a rose too.

5
JULY

Cloudy Days and Sunny Days

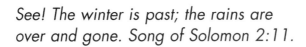

See! The winter is past; the rains are over and gone. Song of Solomon 2:11.

Do you love storms? I love the thunder and lightning, the pouring rain or thickly falling snow. In many parts of the world it rains or snows in the winter. It rained in the Bible lands where Solomon lived. In this verse one person is telling another to look outside and see that winter is over and the weather is clearing up. It's time to go for a hike.

I love winter and the snow it brings, but I certainly am glad when the spring and summer arrive and the skies begin to clear. The dark skies and rain of winter can help us appreciate the summer even more.

Sometimes our day can be sad and dark like a winter day. If someone we love is sick or dies, or someone we know hasn't been very nice to us, it can be like a dark day in winter. But God will bring us sunnier days. Those dark days can help us enjoy and appreciate the sunny days even more. Keep looking to Jesus. If today is a dark, sad day for you, don't worry. Jesus loves you and He'll make the sun shine again.

Beautiful Spots

Descend from the crest of Amana, from the top of Senir, the summit of Hermon, from the lions' dens and the mountain haunts of the leopards. Song of Solomon 4:8.

W e're on a night hike. We're on a night hike because we're looking for a leopard. We would never do this alone. That's why we have a special guide and several others to protect us. Are you wondering why we're looking for a leopard at night? It's because the leopard is a nocturnal animal. Nocturnal animals usually hunt for dinner at night and sleep during the day. That's just the opposite of what most humans do, isn't it?

The leopard is such a beautiful animal, with its yellowish fur and black spots. The problem is that most people will never see how beautiful leopards are because they come out only at night, in secret.

Some people live their lives in secret like the leopard. They don't want anyone to know what they're doing. Sometimes it's because they know the things they're doing are not right.

Jesus doesn't want us to live our lives in secret. He wants our characters to be even more beautiful than a leopard's fur. Don't hide behind sin. Let Jesus change you and shine His beauty through you in the bright sunshine of each new day.

7 JULY

More Than Melons

The Daughter of Zion is left like a shelter in a vineyard, like a hut in a field of melons, like a city under siege. Isaiah 1:8.

We sure need our hiking boots today. It's pretty dirty out here in this hot, dusty field of melons. Actually, what this verse calls melons may actually be what we call cucumbers today. And why would you have a hut in a field of melons? There's one right in front of us. Let's go in, and I'll explain why it's here.

There we go. There's certainly more shade in here. You see, back in the time of the Bible, melons had to be taken care of. They needed to be weeded, turned so they would grow evenly, and watched so that animals and insects wouldn't eat them all before the workers came to harvest them. If no one watched them, they'd probably be ruined. Someone had to stay in the field and watch them the whole growing season. Wow, what a lot of care went into raising melons.

Did you know that God cares for you even more than that? He's always watching over you. That's His job, and He loves it. He loves it because He loves you. What a loving God we have. One who loves us more than melons.

198

Braggin' Ankles

The Lord says, "The women of Zion are haughty, walking along with outstretched necks, flirting with their eyes, tripping along with mincing steps, with ornaments jingling on their ankles. Isaiah 3:16.

Today's verse mentions something that's pretty important to a hike. They're your ankles. If your ankles are broken, you can't hike. If your ankles are sore, you won't want to hike. It's true, your ankles are very important to hiking.

But today's verse is talking about more than just hiking with your ankles. It's talking about bragging with your ankles. How's that. Isaiah 3:16 tells us that your ankles, your eyes, and even the way you walk can be used to show off and try to make people believe you're better than they are. God doesn't want us to be like that. He sent His only Son as a humble servant to die for our sins. If Jesus humbled Himself for us, we should humble ourselves for Him and others.

When you and I think we're better than others, we can't help them, they can't help us, and most important, God has a hard time teaching us anything. Take Isaiah's advice—use your ankles for hiking, not bragging. Humble yourself and serve those around you. Be like Jesus and help others hike right into His arms.

Bald and Beautiful

The Lord will make their scalps bald. Isaiah 3:17.

I want you to stop hiking for just a minute and feel the top of your head. Go ahead—run your fingers along the very top of your head and notice what it feels like. Is it smooth? Is it bumpy? When I feel the top of my head it reminds me of the waves of the ocean. My head is bumpy.

My father has a very bald head. It's OK, because he looks good bald. He tells me that "God made some people with perfect heads, and He gave hair to all the others." Well, my dad might be right. I still have my hair, and the top of my head isn't very smooth. My father always wears a hat on his bald head to protect it from the sun. I guess if I ever go bald I'll wear a hat too. Then no one will see my less than perfect head.

Like my bumpy head, you and I aren't very perfect. We make many mistakes each day. I'm so glad that Jesus loves us anyway. He loved us so much that "while we were still sinners," He died for us. Wear your hat today to protect your head from the sun, and thank Jesus He saved you with a crown of thorns on His head.

Clean as a Paintbrush

As the terebinth and oak leave stumps when they are cut down, so the holy seed will be the stump in the land. Isaiah 6:13.

Today we're hiking through the forest. Do you smell that? It's a very strong odor. Look to your right. I think it's coming from that tree. Look at that thick, yellowish stuff draining out. Do you know what tree this is? It's a terebinth tree. That's what the people in Bible times used to make turpentine from. What's turpentine? I'm glad you asked.

I love to paint pictures with oil paints. They really are oily, and they take a long time to dry. And when it's time to wash your brush out, don't use water. Oil and water just won't mix. I use turpentine. It's strong-smelling, but it's one of the only things that will clean oil paint out of a brush.

Sometimes your parents may need to be as strong as turpentine with you. When you've done something wrong, they may need to discipline you in a way that hurts. Remember this: They want to guide you in the right way—and they want to help you get all the gunk out of your life, just like turpentine gets oil paint out of a brush.

11 JULY

An Eclipse of the Heart

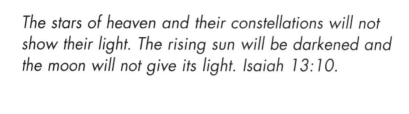

The stars of heaven and their constellations will not show their light. The rising sun will be darkened and the moon will not give its light. Isaiah 13:10.

Well, isn't it a lovely day to be hiking? Not a cloud in the sky. Wait, why is it turning dark? There aren't any clouds. It's not time for the sun to go down. It's an eclipse! The moon is moving right between the earth and the sun. And it's getting dark. Wow, this is amazing! Did you know an eclipse can also happen at night? It's true. When the earth moves directly between the sun and the moon, the moon goes dark; that's because the moon depends on the sun for its light.

Some days it can seem as if there's an eclipse in our heart. It seems as if something has moved between God's love and us. But don't you believe it for one minute. Romans 8:39 says, "Neither height nor depth, nor anything else in all creation, will be able to separate us from the love of God that is in Christ Jesus our Lord." Nothing can separate us from God's love. The earth can separate the sun from the moon so the moon won't even light up, but nothing can ever, ever separate us from God's love.

Don't Laugh Now

Hyenas will howl in her strongholds, jackals in her luxurious palaces. Her time is at hand, and her days will not be prolonged. Isaiah 13:22.

Careful now—we're hiking in dangerous territory today. It's the place of the hyenas. Hyenas are powerful members of the dog family who hunt at night and look for weak and injured animals to prey on. One type of hyena even "laughs" when it catches its victims—at least it sounds like it's laughing. If it were smart, it wouldn't laugh, though. Lions hear them laughing and then come to steal their catch. Why do I not feel sorry for the hyena?

Satan is a lot like those hyenas. He hunts for the souls of God's people. I think he probably laughs when he causes us to sin and fall away from God. But he shouldn't laugh. God hears and comes to rescue us. He's the "Lion of the Tribe of Judah," and He's always there to help us out of our worst sins.

Hiking in Satan's territory is dangerous. We should stay as far away as possible. But we should always remember that Jesus is a strong lion who will always come to save us when we're in trouble. Watch out, Satan—don't laugh now.

13 JULY

A Deadly Bite

An oracle concerning the animals of the Negev: Through a land of hardship and distress, of lions and lionesses, of adders and darting snakes. Isaiah 30:6.

Adders and darting snakes—does that scare you? It does me—especially the part about the adder. Some adders are very poisonous snakes. There are many kinds of adders, but the scariest is the death adder. It lives in Australia and hides under leaves and branches during the day. At night it comes out and looks for lizards and rodents to eat. When it finds a lizard to eat, it coils up, strikes, and sinks its fangs into the lizard. It injects a venom that paralyzes the poor little animal and makes its blood go thick. Ooh, that's terrible, isn't it?

There are things in life that are that deadly too. Drugs, cigarettes, and alcohol can all kill. When they get into your body they don't want to let you go. They also do terrible things to your blood and the organs inside your body.

Making good choices about your health is important. It's important because when we can't think clearly, we can't hear God speaking to us through our conscience.

Keep the bad stuff out of your body. Don't let it bite you and keep you away from God.

Families in the Air

The owl will nest there and lay eggs, she will hatch them, and care for her young under the shadow of her wings; there also the falcons will gather, each with its mate. Isaiah 34:15.

Hike quietly now. Look up into the sky—right there along the edge of the cliff. Do you see that bird flying swiftly next to the rock? That's a falcon. Isn't it a beautiful bird? Look now—he's turning and landing right on that little ledge. Oh, look—there's the mommy falcon and their little baby falcons in that nest.

I think we like to see animal families together in nature, because we know that's the way God intended families to be. Unfortunately, not all moms and dads and children are together. It's sad when that happens. But you can do something right now to keep the family you have together.

Whoever your family is, you can do something to help make it the happiest family it can be. You can love and respect and help one another. You can pray for and with one another. God wants us to teach one another what He is like, by showing our families how much we love them. Do something special, and show your family today you love them with all your heart.

15 JULY

Nervous Knees

Strengthen the feeble hands, steady the knees that give way. Isaiah 35:3.

Have you ever been nervous or seen someone who was? Maybe they were nervous about getting up in front of a lot of people. Maybe they were sweating or shaking. Maybe their knees were knocking together. Our brains make our bodies do funny things when we're nervous.

Why is it that some people can get up in front of a large crowd without feeling nervous and others won't even try it? It's a thing our brains do called worry. We think about what will happen if we say the wrong thing or if we trip and fall or do something silly. God doesn't want us to spend our lives worrying about getting up in front of a crowd of people or about anything else. He wants us to trust in Him. He is the one, as Isaiah tells us in today's verse, who can even keep our knees from knocking.

Whatever you are worried about today or tomorrow or the next day—choose to let God worry about it. He created the whole world, and He can take care of our worries, too. Trust in Him, and your knees will stop knocking.

Do You Have Thick Skin?

I have dug wells in foreign lands and drunk the water there. With the soles of my feet I have dried up all the streams of Egypt. Isaiah 37:25.

Ouch, ouch! We're hiking in the great outdoors without our hiking boots today. The soles of our feet are just not tough enough, are they? Well, ours might not be tough, but some people's are.

I remember the boy who lived next door to me when I was about 14. I had grown up in the city with my shoes on. He had grown up in the country with his shoes off. He almost never wore shoes. He could walk over sticks, rocks, and cornfields without his shoes. I tried it once—I'll never do that again. It hurt! The reason that boy's soles were so tough was that he had developed very thick skin on his feet.

You and I have to develop "thick skin." Sometimes people will say nasty things to us and hurt our feelings. But rather than saying something to hurt them back, Paul tells us in 1 Corinthians 13 that we must love them. That's what I mean by developing a "thick skin." The next time someone does something that hurts you, remember the soles of your feet. Develop thick skin, and love them back!

Moving Swiftly for God

I cried like a swift or thrush, I moaned like a mourning dove. My eyes grew weak as I looked to the heavens. I am troubled; O Lord, come to my aid!" Isaiah 38:14.

Whoa! Look out! What was that? There it is again. It's so fast. What we've discovered on our hike today is a bird called the swift—and that's the right name for sure. This bird is the fastest of all small birds. It darts and weaves and dives. It feeds, drinks, bathes, and even looks for a husband or wife—all while flying. Sometimes it flies all night. It hardly ever stops moving.

There's a story in the Bible about a man named Gideon. Gideon had to choose some men to defend Israel. He told them to get some water from the stream. Some men stopped, got down on their knees, and drank. The men who scooped the water up as they ran were the men God wanted to go into battle for Him. He knew they would always be alert. He knew they would always be moving for Him.

God wants us to be on the move for Him. He wants us to tell others about Him every day through our words and actions. Can you move "swiftly" today and let others know about the God you serve?

Help, I'm Caught!

Your sons have fainted; they lie at the head of every street, like antelope caught in a net. They are filled with the wrath of the Lord and the rebuke of your God. Isaiah 51:20.

Today we're hiking through the wilderness of the land of Israel. Wait, do you hear that thrashing sound? Over there—it's caught in the net. It's an antelope. Someone has set up a net to catch something, and they've caught an antelope. That's about the only way you can catch an antelope. They are so fast. Antelope are similar to deer, and they roam through the fields eating grass. Most have sharp horns on their head.

Today's verse talks about people who hate God. It says they're like an antelope caught in a net. Can you think of what that might mean? I think it's talking about sinners being caught in a net of sin. Many people think that God just wants to keep us from having fun, so He makes many rules. Actually, God's laws keep us out of trouble. They keep us from getting caught in the net of sin.

Obey God today. He really knows what He's talking about. He really wants to keep us from the trap of sin. He really cares for you and me.

19
JULY

I Don't Like Spiders and Snakes

No one calls for justice; no one pleads his case with integrity. They rely on empty arguments and speak lies; they conceive trouble and give birth to evil. They hatch the eggs of vipers and spin a spider's web. Whoever eats their eggs will die, and when one is broken, an adder is hatched. Isaiah 59:4, 5.

I have to be honest. Today's verse does not sound very good, does it? It talks about those who lie and want to trap others in their lies. On our very long hike so far this year, we've seen snakes and spiders. Today's verse talks about snake eggs and spiderwebs. Although snakes are very good to have around (because they eat many rats and mice), and spiders help us out by catching many flies in their webs, most people just don't like spiders and snakes.

Today's verse says that people who lie and deceive are like spiders and snakes. They try to trap and hurt others in their lies. They want others to be a part of their web of deceit, and inject their poison into them. Always be kind and gentle to those around you. Don't get too close to those who lie and cheat. Stay focused on Jesus and don't get bitten.

Living Leaves

All of us have become like one who is unclean, and all our righteous acts are like filthy rags; we all shrivel up like a leaf, and like the wind our sins sweep us away. Isaiah 64:6.

For some of you reading this, today's hike will be in the middle of the summer. For some of you it will be in the middle of winter. It just depends on which side of the world you live. Today, however, I want to talk about the fall. Fall is my favorite time of year.

Today's verse talks about what happens to leaves in the fall. It says they shrivel up. The bad thing about today's verse is that we are like those shriveled leaves. It tells us that sin has a hold on us. What can we do?

The only thing we can do is to give ourselves to Jesus. He is the great tree doctor. He can bring new life to our souls. He can turn our shriveled lives into lives that bless others. He can keep us from being blown away by sin. Ask Jesus to come into your heart once again today or maybe even for the very first time. He'll make you into a tree that's green and beautiful, blessing others and giving honor to Him all year long.

Stolen Eggs

Like a partridge that hatches eggs it did not lay is the man who gains riches by unjust means. When his life is half gone, they will desert him, and in the end he will prove to be a fool. Jeremiah 17:11.

Do you hear it—that low whistle? Wait a minute. I know who that is—it's Mr. Quail. A quail is a bird that is often called a partridge, and by the sounds of today's verse he's got a mean streak. It seems Mr. Quail Partridge is a bit of a thief. He's stolen eggs that another bird laid. But today's verse also says that things don't turn out too well for Mr. Partridge. The eggs he stole from another bird will hatch. The children he thought he had will leave him. He'll be a lonely Mr. Partridge after all.

Our Bible says that being a thief just isn't worth it. Some people steal because they think they just have to have more things. But those things will leave them. Most people who steal get caught; they lose others' respect; they end up without friends and very lonely. Always be honest. Don't take what belongs to someone else. God will give you all the blessings you need.

Quite the Bite

Egypt is a beautiful heifer, but a gadfly is coming against her from the north. Jeremiah 46:20.

Ouch, did you feel that? Look at that bite—it's huge. Look at that fly—it's even larger. Where are we hiking today? Well, we just happen to be in Egypt, one of Israel's neighbors to the south, and we just happen to be out in a field with the cows. These huge biting flies we see are called horseflies, or gadflies. Today's verse calls Egypt a beautiful heifer. A heifer is the mama cow, which is actually saying the same thing, but, oh well. It says that a gadfly, or a horsefly, is coming to get mama. Gadflies can get mean. The female gadfly actually sucks the blood right out of the cow. Ouch—don't let them get near you!

God wasn't just talking about flies here. He meant that another nation was coming to attack Egypt because they had been disobedient. God's laws are really good for us. He only gives them to protect us. If Egypt had obeyed God, they would have had a much happier life. Gadflies probably won't bite you, but Satan wants to bite you with temptation. Obey God today. His laws are for your happiness. Stay away from the bite of sin.

Freezin' Folks

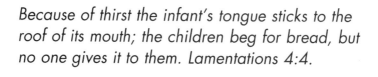

Because of thirst the infant's tongue sticks to the roof of its mouth; the children beg for bread, but no one gives it to them. Lamentations 4:4.

Has your tongue ever stuck to the roof of your mouth? The poor baby in today's verse is so thirsty and dry; its tongue is sticking to the roof of its mouth. That poor baby is suffering so badly.

I hope the roof of your mouth is never that dry, but I can teach you a little trick about your tongue and the roof of your mouth. Have you ever eaten ice cream too quickly? What happens? Does your head hurt? Does it feel like your brain is freezing? Quickly, put your tongue on the roof of your mouth—you'll feel better faster. It's because your tongue warms up the roof of your mouth and gets the temperature of the blood flowing through your head back to where it should be.

Sometimes people can be as cold as ice cream. Sometimes people can be downright mean to each other. As a follower of Jesus you can warm things up. Always be kind, friendly, and helpful to those around you. If you are a warm person, you can slowly but surely warm up those "freezin' folks" around you.

Dirty Rubies

Their princes were brighter than snow and whiter than milk, their bodies more ruddy than rubies, their appearance like sapphires. But now they are blacker than soot; they are not recognized in the streets. Their skin has shriveled on their bones; it has become as dry as a stick. Lamentations 4:7, 8.

Their princes were . . . more ruddy than rubies." That's what today's verse says. As we hike through the streets today, though, we see that now "they are blacker than soot." Too bad, so sad. How did God's people go from being so pretty to being so dirty? How could they go from being as precious as a ruby, a very valuable stone, to being so filthy? It's because they put themselves first and left God out of the picture.

God wants us to put Him first. It's not because He just wants attention. It's because He knows if we put ourselves or other things first, we'll just get into trouble. So often we think we know what's best for us, but only God knows that. Only He can lead us on life's hike and get us safely to heaven. I want to be hiking in heaven someday, don't you? Put God first in your life, and you will be enjoying heaven's nature hikes forever and ever!

Turn Your Eyes Upon Jesus

Moreover, our eyes failed, looking in vain for help; from our towers we watched for a nation that could not save us. Lamentations 4:17.

Do you wear glasses? Do you know anyone who wears glasses or contacts? Sin has caused things to go bad, including people's eyes. Some must wear glasses to correct the problem they have with their eyes. I'm 43 years old as I'm writing today. I haven't had to wear glasses until recently. When I read small letters, they seem to be fuzzy and difficult to read. I use reading glasses to help me now.

Today's verse talks about another kind of eye problem. These people had eye problems because they were looking for help in the wrong place. They were looking for a nation to save them. The truth is that only God can save us. We should always turn to Him. When times are good and when times are bad He can always set our hiking boots on the right trail. Don't let your eyes fail you by looking to people or money or anything else to save you. Turn your eyes upon Jesus—He can fix your eye problems and keep you on the heavenly path.

I Can See Right Through You

This was the appearance and structure of the wheels: They sparkled like chrysolite, and all four looked alike. Each appeared to be made like a wheel intersecting a wheel. Ezekiel 1:16.

Isn't it a beautiful day? The sun is shining. And here we are hiking along this lovely path looking at all the—stop! Look at that beautiful stone sitting right on the path in front of us. We almost stepped on it. It's greenish and crystal clear. I know what this stone is—it's chrysolite. Chrysolite is a very pretty, olive-green stone. It isn't always crystal clear like the one we've found, though. Sometimes there are other objects inside the stone, and sometimes it's all cracked inside. Those things happened when the chrysolite was being formed many years ago.

Jesus wants us to be crystal clear, just like the stone we've found today. He wants our lives to be pure and clean. People should be able to "see right through us." That means we're always honest with others. We always tell the truth. That can happen only when we turn our eyes on Jesus like we talked about yesterday. Let Jesus form you into His image today, and be a crystal-clear Christian for Him.

27 JULY

Two Peas in a Pod

Take wheat and barley, beans and lentils, millet and spelt; put them in a storage jar and use them to make bread for yourself. You are to eat it during the 390 days you lie on your side. Ezekiel 4:9.

Have you ever eaten lentils? Maybe you've had lentil stew or lentil loaf or even lentil soup. I really like lentils. If you cook them with a little bit of garlic, they taste good, and they're really good for you.

Do you know how lentils grow? Hike right over here and I'll show you. Lentils grow in bushy plants about 12 inches high. The lentil seeds, the little things you eat, grow in pairs in little pods. There's a saying that goes, "You two are like two peas in a pod." Well, lentils belong to the pea family, so maybe the person who said that first was actually talking about lentils. It means you're the best of friends with someone—you're just alike.

Do you have a best friend? If so, why don't you tell them how much you love and appreciate them today? If you don't have a best friend, be the best friend you can be to someone who really needs a friend. See how much fun it is to be "two peas in a pod."

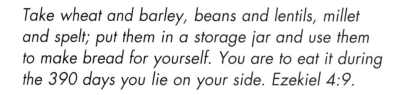

Get Ready for This One

"Very well," he said, "I will let you bake your bread over cow manure." Ezekiel 4:15.

We're going to step very carefully through today's verse. It's about cow manure. Why would God put cow manure in the Bible? He was trying to teach Israel an important lesson, and believe it or not, there are lessons we can learn from cow manure, too.

You see, God's people had been disobedient again. God had to teach them a lesson. Usually the Israelites would bake their bread over a fire made with wood, but an army was surrounding the city and no one could get out to collect any wood. The only thing left to burn was cow manure. Now, I really wouldn't want to use cow manure to bake my bread, but if I was really hungry, I guess I'd have to.

God doesn't like to punish, but sometimes He must to teach His people lessons. But even though He sometimes punishes, He always gives us what we need. It may not be what we like, but He won't let us starve. I'm so thankful God teaches us the lessons of life and that He always supplies our needs.

Jesus in Your Heart

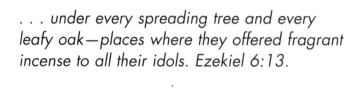

. . . under every spreading tree and every leafy oak—places where they offered fragrant incense to all their idols. Ezekiel 6:13.

Let's hike to that oak tree over there and rest awhile. Ah, that's better. The shade is nice, isn't it? What's this broken stone? Let me tell you a sad story of long ago.

When the ancient people of Israel lived here, they disobeyed God. They began to worship the gods of other nations. Believe it or not, they even built stone gods and bowed down to them. Do you think that a hunk of stone could do anything for you? Do you think you could love a hunk of stone or that it could love you? Of course not—but that's exactly what many of God's people began to believe. It's a very sad story.

You and I can do things differently today. We can make sure we don't worship other gods. No, I don't mean that you and I would bow down to stone gods. But we can let other things take God's place. Television, sports, and even going to church can take the place of really getting to know Jesus. Get to know Him today, love Him with all your heart, and never let anything take the place of Jesus.

Cords of Love

On the day you were born your cord was not cut. Ezekiel 16:4.

Today we've hiked right into one of the most wonderful experiences in life. Do you know what that is? A baby is being born! Look at the cute little baby. He's still attached to his mother by a cord. It's called the umbilical cord. All the blood and food and vitamins and minerals that the baby needed for nine months while he was growing inside his mommy came right through that cord. God is so amazing to have created us in such a wonderful way.

Did you know that God wants us to always be attached to Him? Oh, not through an umbilical cord, but a cord of life and love. All the strength and love and care we need to grow into healthy Christians come right from God. If we don't stay connected to Him, our Christian life will die.

Satan will try to disconnect us from God, but don't let him do that. God will never let you go—make sure you don't let Him go. Keep your eyes on Jesus and always stay close to Him through His cords of love.

Sour Grapes

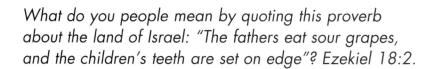

What do you people mean by quoting this proverb about the land of Israel: "The fathers eat sour grapes, and the children's teeth are set on edge"? Ezekiel 18:2.

Today we're hiking right next to a fence. That doesn't seem like such a great thing, but it's what's growing on that fence that I like. They're grapes! Here, try one. Oh, wait—I should warn you that these aren't the kind of grapes you buy in the grocery store. They're wild grapes, and they are sour! Personally, I like sour grapes, but not everyone does. Today's verse is really telling the truth when it says that sour grapes set people's teeth on edge.

There's a saying that talks about "sour grapes." We say someone is eating sour grapes when they don't get their way and then say they didn't want it anyway. They're just trying to cover up. They're really whining a little.

I love wild grapes, but I don't think we should be like sour grapes. Jesus wants us to be cheerful witnesses for Him. He wants us to be honest and happy people who bring light and life to everyone around us. Eat lots of fruit today. Just don't throw those sour grapes at others.

It Lasts and Lasts and Lasts

1 AUGUST

Of oaks from Bashan they made your oars; of cypress wood from the coasts of Cyprus they made your deck, inlaid with ivory. Ezekiel 27:6.

Clean off your hiking boots. Try not to get the deck of the ship dirty. It's made of cypress wood. Doesn't it smell good?

Cypress is a special kind of wood with a very strong smell. It smells that way because it has very strong chemicals in it. The strong chemicals in cypress wood resist the water that rots most other woods and even acid that would eat away at other trees.

A cypress tree called the Tree of Tule is one of the largest trees in the world. It's about 175 feet around the trunk and 150 feet tall—that's huge! Scientists believe that tree is between 3,000 and 5,000 years old. Amazing!

But I can tell you about something that's even bigger than the Tree of Tule and lasts even longer. It's God's love. The Bible tells us that nothing can ever take God's love away from us. He'll love us forever, and there's nothing bigger than His love for us. Aren't you thankful that Someone loves you that much? I sure am!

What Big Teeth You Have

The men of Rhodes traded with you, and many coastlands were your customers; they paid you with ivory tusks and ebony. Ezekiel 27:15.

Careful, now—you don't want him to charge you. Today we're hiking in Africa and visiting elephants. Look at those long, curved white teeth sticking out of the top part of the elephant's mouth. They actually are teeth, although we call them tusks. Those tusks are made of the same kind of material your teeth are made of. Because they're so large and pure white inside, and because there aren't that many elephants around the world, people consider ivory tusks to be very valuable. They're so valuable that people have hunted and killed elephants to cut off their tusks and sell the ivory. There are laws now that protect the elephants from this kind of treatment. I'm so glad.

I know something that's even more valuable than ivory. It's Jesus—and we never have to worry about stealing Him for ourselves. He's always there to hear everyone's prayers and help all people every day. Aren't you glad we have the most valuable Person in the whole world to love us?

Are You Minty Today?

Judah and Israel traded with you; they exchanged wheat from Minnith and confections, honey, oil and balm for your wares. Ezekiel 27:17.

This is such a noisy place, isn't it? We've hiked right into an outdoor market. Each person has brought something to trade with someone else. That man over there brought some clothes he made, that man brought animals, that woman brought pottery, and that man brought balm. What's balm, you say? Balm is the oil from the leaves of certain plants. It has a very strong smell and is used to make tea, flavor soup, and even fruit drinks. Most balm comes from the oil of different kinds of mint plants, and it sure is tasty.

God wants you to be a balm today. He wants you to make life taste better for the people around you. He wants you to sweeten that sad neighbor. He wants you to calm down your angry friend with your beautiful smile. God has given us so many good things. We can be so thankful for them. They should make us so happy that we want to make life taste better for everyone. Be a balm for God and act a little minty today.

I'm Holdin' You Up

Danites and Greeks from Uzal bought your merchandise; they exchanged wrought iron, cassia, and calamus for your wares. Ezekiel 27:19.

Look at this. We've hiked right into the middle of more trading today. One of the things that's being traded today is calamus. Calamus comes from a type of palm tree called the rattan. It has long leaves that look like swords, and believe it or not, they use the leaves, especially their stems, to make furniture. Imagine that. You could make a rattan-palm-leaf chair that would hold you up. One rattan leaf couldn't do it, two couldn't do it, but if you weave many of them together in the right way, a whole group of them could support your entire body.

Christians are like that. We need one another. We need to support one another and hold one another up. There isn't one of us who can tell the whole world about Jesus, but if we all work together and each of us tells the people we know about Him, very soon the whole world could know about the wonderful love of God. Tell someone about Jesus today and hold one another up. Together we make a great team.

Got Your Sword Today?

Consider Assyria, once a cedar in Lebanon, with beautiful branches overshadowing the forest; it towered on high, its top above the thick foliage. Ezekiel 31:3.

About four months ago we hiked through the cedars of Lebanon. We talked about how rot-resistant and bug-repelling they were. Cedar trees also have huge leafy tops that shade the entire forest.

There are other forests on our earth that have huge leafy tops. The rain forests in South America are like that. They're called rain forests because it rains so much there. You'll find rain forests in countries like Brazil. Because it rains so much, the rain forest grows thick. You can't even walk through it without a big knife called a machete to chop all the leaves and vines out of the way.

Life can be like that sometimes. Satan tries to put many things in our way each day to discourage us. Have you ever heard the Bible called a sword? Ephesians 6:17 calls the Bible the sword of the Spirit. The Bible is like a big machete cutting through the rain forest of life. God's Word can cut through all of life's problems. Pick up your sword today and let God clear your path.

Slippery Is Good

You are also to provide with it morning by morning a grain offering, consisting of a sixth of an ephah with a third of a hin of oil to moisten the flour. The presenting of this grain offering to the Lord is a lasting ordinance. Ezekiel 46:14.

It's a good thing we have our hiking boots on today. We're in slippery territory. Our little trip takes us to an oil press. The men are squeezing the oil right out of the corn. That's amazing.

Do you know what oil is? There are many different kinds of oil that come from many different places, but they all do pretty much the same thing. They make things go smoothly. You'll find oil in olives, corn, sunflower seeds, under the ground, and thousands of other places. God sure did create a lot of oil for us to use.

God wants you to be a little oily too. He wants you to help things go smoothly all around you. By your example and your words, you can help smooth out an argument, you can help a teacher's day go more smoothly, you can help your parents around the house and make things smoother for them. Get a little oily today and be a smoother for God.

Stargazing

7 AUGUST

The king summoned the magicians, enchanters, sorcerers, and astrologers to tell him what he had dreamed. When they came in and stood before the king, he said to them, "I have had a dream that troubles me and I want to know what it means." Daniel 2:2, 3.

Now, tie up those bootlaces and look alive—we're in King Nebuchadnezzar's court today. Shh—he's called in all his wise men. Look, he's even called the astrologers. This must be pretty important. Listen now, the king is speaking. He's telling them he's had a dream and he wants them to tell him what it was. How are they going to do that? Only God knows stuff like that.

How about those astrologers? Do you know what they do? They look at the stars and say they know what's going to happen tomorrow. Well, I've got news for them. They need to look just a little past those stars up there to our God. He's the one who really knows the future.

Did you know there are still people today who look to the stars and think they'll find the future? What a silly thing to do. I'm so thankful we have a God who really does know the future. Stick with Him. He'll let you in on a few secrets.

Have You Lost Your Mind?

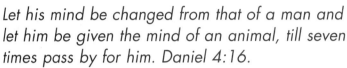

Let his mind be changed from that of a man and let him be given the mind of an animal, till seven times pass by for him. Daniel 4:16.

Yuou're going to see the most amazing thing on our hike today. Do you remember yesterday's story when King Nebuchadnezzar called in the astrologers so they could tell him what his dream had been the night before? Well, the old king should have been asking God what his dream was. He just never gave God the credit, and now look at him. That's the king out there in the field with long hair, walking on his hands and knees, and howling like an animal. He's even got the mind of an animal.

There's a big difference between the mind or brain that you and I have, and the mind of an animal. Just look at the king! God gave us a mind that could think through problems and decide on answers. Most important, our minds can make a decision to love Jesus.

God gave animals instincts. That means they just do what they do without really thinking about it. You and I are different. We can think, and we can choose. Choose to say yes to God's gift of eternal life, and let's have a meeting of the minds in heaven someday.

Cut Those Nails

Immediately what had been said about Nebuchadnezzar was fulfilled. He was driven away from people and ate grass like cattle. His body was drenched with the dew of heaven until his hair grew like the feathers of an eagle and his nails like the claws of a bird. Daniel 4:33.

I told you that was the king! I know you didn't want to believe me, but that's him, all right. Look at his fingernails. Today's verse says they were like the claws of a bird. Let me tell you about the amazing claws of a bird called the woodpecker. Have you ever seen a man in your backyard with special boots climbing up your telephone pole? Well, Mr. Woodpecker just climbs straight up the side of the tree without wearing any boots at all. It's all because God gave him special claws. What a talented bird.

God gave you talents also. Maybe you play an instrument very well. Maybe schoolwork is very easy for you. Maybe you can build things better than most. You can be glad God gave you those talents, but more important, you can use them for Him. When people say, "You are so talented," just say, "Jesus made me this way." Give Him all the praise and lead others to know Him too.

Sweet Dreams

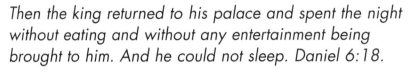

Then the king returned to his palace and spent the night without eating and without any entertainment being brought to him. And he could not sleep. Daniel 6:18.

Well, I should say the king should have trouble sleeping. Go ahead, when you're done reading this today, read what happened in Daniel 6. King Darius let some sneaky guys talk him into making a silly law that ended up putting Daniel in a den of hungry lions. If you had done that to one of your friends, I think you'd have trouble sleeping too.

Did you know some people have trouble sleeping every night? It's called insomnia. There are many reasons people can't go to sleep at night, but today I want to tell you about just one of them. It's worry. Sometimes people have trouble sleeping because they are worrying about what will happen to them, how they will pay all their bills, or about something they've done to get themselves in trouble.

God wants us to know that He can take care of all our problems. He is the great problem fixer. He knows all the answers and all the solutions. Don't spend your time worrying about the things in your life you can't fix. Let God do the worrying for you, and have sweet dreams tonight!

Bear Jealousy

There before me was a second beast, which looked like a bear. It was raised up on one of its sides, and it had three ribs in its mouth between its teeth. It was told, "Get up and eat your fill of flesh!" Daniel 7:5.

It's a long way off, but if you look very closely you can see a bear. She has cubs, too. Now let's turn our hiking boots right around and head out of here. We don't want mama bear to smell us and discover we're here. That would spell disaster. Why would that be such a problem? you say. Don't mothers like to show off their babies? Well, human mamas do, but not mama bears. They are very protective, and if anyone comes near their little cubs, they attack.

The bear that Daniel was telling us about in this verse represented a king that lived long ago. He attacked many countries and had many victories. Sadly, many people died in the wars this bear started.

It's so sad that many people still die in wars all over the world today. The Bible tells us when we see all these wars, it means that Jesus will be coming back soon. Let's pray for wars to stop and Jesus to come. For me, that would be the perfect victory.

Red Tide

Because of this the land mourns, and all who live in it waste away; the beasts of the field and the birds of the air and the fish of the sea are dying. Hosea 4:3.

It's so nice hiking by the ocean today. To hear the waves crashing into shore, to smell the salt in the air, to see the red water and dying fish—wait a minute, what's happening? Why is the water that reddish color and why are all the fish dying?

The water turns that color when there is too much red algae. It's called a "red tide." Algae are little animals that live in the water all the time, but there aren't usually that many of them all in one place. This red algae also puts out poison that kills the fish.

It's sad to say but our world of sin is like the red tide. If you and I give in to just a little of Satan's pollution, it can grow until it takes over our lives and begins to kill our friendship with God. I'm glad to say that God is much more powerful than Satan and can take away the sin and pollution from our lives. Let's decide to stick close to God and not give in to Satan's garbage.

Popular Under the Poplars

They sacrifice on the mountaintops and burn offerings on the hills, under oak, poplar, and terebinth, where the shade is pleasant. Hosea 4:13.

If you're reading this in the United States of America, summer is now in full swing. It's a warm day, so let's hike right under the shade of that poplar tree. I just love big shady trees in the summertime, don't you? Actually, poplar trees are a big family of trees. I live in Colorado and love the cottonwood and quaking aspen trees here. They're both members of the poplar family.

Unfortunately, back in ancient Israel, God's people used poplar trees for more than just shade. Today's verse says they sacrificed burnt offerings. The sad thing was that those offerings weren't to the God of heaven. They were sacrifices to other gods. Israel was doing what was popular under the poplars. That means they were following the crowd. They were doing what others were doing without really thinking for themselves.

God wants you and me to think for ourselves. He doesn't want us to do what everyone else is doing, just because everyone else is doing it. Stand up and do the right thing for Jesus. Don't worry about being popular under the poplars.

Band-Aids

Come, let us return to the Lord. He has torn us to pieces but he will heal us; he has injured us but he will bind up our wounds. Hosea 6:1.

Have you ever received a spanking? Most children have. Do you think your parents enjoyed giving you spankings? Many children might say yes, but it's really not true. Moms and dads really don't like to punish their children, but they know it has to be done for their children to learn the hard lessons of life.

Today's verse talks about the punishment God must give His people at times. He doesn't actually tear us apart like the verse says. The writer was saying it that way to help us understand that punishment hurts. It also says that God will bind up our wounds. He won't let us bleed too much. Just as losing too much blood can cause a person to die, God knows we need only enough tough lessons to help us return to Him.

Jesus bled at the cross and died so you and I wouldn't have to lose our blood and be away from God forever. I'm so glad we have a kind Father in heaven who puts Band-Aids on our hurts and heals our hearts, aren't you?

Beautiful Inside and Out

Israel was a spreading vine; he brought forth fruit for himself. As his fruit increased, he built more altars; as his land prospered, he adorned his sacred stones. Hosea 10:1.

It's so nice to go on a nature hike, isn't it? You can see so many wonderful things. Some are very beautiful. Some aren't so beautiful. Looks can be deceiving, though. Some of the things that look very nice turn out to be not so nice. For instance, have you ever seen or touched poison ivy?

Poison ivy can be like the spreading vine in today's verse. Poison ivy has such beautiful leaves and pretty little berries, but don't touch it! It gives most people a terribly sore, itching rash with white blisters. Ouch and yuck! Don't get near it!

Our verse says the people of Israel were like a spreading vine, just like poison ivy. They even had fruit. That means it looked like everything was going OK. But in their hearts, things weren't OK. They built altars to other gods. They weren't being faithful at all. Remember, God looks into a person's heart to see if they are following Him. Ask Him to clean the sin from your heart today. He'll make you as beautiful on the inside as you are on the outside.

Keep Your Word and Kill the Weeds

They make many promises, take false oaths and make agreements; therefore lawsuits spring up like poisonous weeds in a plowed field. Hosea 10:4.

On today's hike we're going to talk about more poisonous plants and weeds. There are many, you know. Some of their names are larkspur, lupines, spotted hemlock, Jimsonweed, Indian hemp, western sneezeweed, corn cockle, ball nettle, bittersweet, black locust, castor bean, and white snakeroot. Many of these plants are so poisonous they will even kill big cows if the cows eat them for lunch. Now, that's powerful.

Today's verse says that when we make promises and don't keep them, all kinds of trouble springs up. A promise is something you tell someone you'll do. When we make promises we should keep them. A promise says we will keep our word. If we go back on promises, people begin to think they can't trust us. When that happens, all kinds of trouble starts and lying weeds begin to grow.

It's sad not to be trusted. It hurts when people think we're lying. It's nice to be believed when you say something. Only make promises you can keep. When you say you'll do something, do it. Keep your word and kill the weeds.

Just a Bunch of Hot Air

Therefore they will be like the morning mist, like the early dew that disappears, like chaff swirling from a threshing floor, like smoke escaping through a window. Hosea 13:3.

Today we're hiking through the desert. Look across the miles of sand. Do you see those heat waves rising? Have you ever watched the smoke of a campfire? Did you notice the smoke rose to the sky? Whenever any air is warmer than the air around it, it rises. That's why hot-air balloons rise into the sky. The hot air is trying to get out and it can't, so the balloon rises into the sky.

What happens to that hot air rising into the sky? It just goes up, never to be seen again. Today's verse talks about people who worship idols and not the true God. God says they will rise up like heat waves and smoke, never to be seen again. That's a sad ending. Their life will be over, because only Jesus can give eternal life.

Jesus wants us to worship Him. He doesn't want us to follow Satan. He knows that Satan's life will end up in smoke. He doesn't want you and me to end up that way. Follow Jesus, and you will rise up to meet Him in the air when He comes again!

Be a Wise Child

*Pains as of a woman in childbirth come to him,
but he is a child without wisdom. Hosea 13:13.*

Did you know you caused your mother a lot of pain? It's true—when you were born, your mother hurt. But as soon as your mother saw you she was so happy all her pain seemed to go away—well, almost. If you have a brother or sister, you might wonder why your mother would go through all that pain more than once. It's because she loves you all so much, of course.

Our verse tells us about someone who isn't very wise. He learns painful lessons, even as painful as childbirth, but soon forgets about the pain and gets into trouble all over again. It was a good thing for your mother to forget about the pain she had when you were born, but it's a bad thing for us to forget the pain of tough lessons.

Jesus wants us to learn from tough lessons. He wants us to remember the trouble we've had so we won't have to go through it again. Learn your lessons well. Don't go through the pain twice. Be a wise child and live a happier life.

Sharp Teeth

A nation has invaded my land, powerful and without number; it has the teeth of a lion, the fangs of a lioness. Joel 1:6.

We're hiking through the wilderness today. We're going to see something that will be hard to watch, but it's part of nature. You'll notice that today's verse talks about a lion and a lioness. It talks about their teeth, or fangs. The lioness hunts for the family's food at night. She crouches in the bushes until dinner walks by. When a deer or other animal walks near, she jumps out of the bushes and (this is the hard-to-watch part) sinks her teeth into the animal's neck. Ouch. It seems so sad, but that's what sin has done to nature.

Today's verse talks about a nation that invaded the land God promised His people. This nation did a lot of damage. They bit into Israel like a lioness bites into an animal's neck. That must have been very painful for God's people. They could have avoided it all if they would have just obeyed God.

God asks us to obey Him because He knows we'll be happiest if we do. He really knows what's best for us and wants us to be happy. Follow God's plan today, and don't get bit by those big teeth.

241

20
AUGUST

Water Your Garden

The seeds are shriveled beneath the clods. The storehouses are in ruins, the granaries have been broken down, for the grain has dried up. Joel 1:17.

Look very carefully as you hike across this dry, dusty field. There, pick up one of those dirt chunks. Do you see it? Right there in the hole. It's a wheat seed. It's not growing up into a wheat plant, though. Seeds need water to grow and there's no water around here. That's the story of today's verse.

Did you know Christians need water to grow too? Yes, we need water for our bodies to grow, but even more, we need the water of the Holy Spirit to grow in Jesus. The Holy Spirit is part of God's family, along with the Father and the Son, Jesus. The Holy Spirit comforts us and teaches us and helps us to know right and wrong. The Holy Spirit is a very important person in our lives as Christians.

Ask God's Holy Spirit to be with you today. Let the Holy Spirit water your life. He'll bring you joy today and keep you from drying up like seeds in a dusty field.

Beautiful Skies, Beautiful Hearts

I will show wonders in the heavens and on the earth, blood and fire and billows of smoke. Joel 2:30.

It's late at night now. Let's hike over to that hilltop so we can see the sky without anything blocking our view. Isn't it beautiful? The stars, the moon, the planets—everything God put into the sky works in such perfect order. They truly are "wonders in the heavens."

Look over there. Do you see that beautiful, colorful, shimmering curtain in the sky? It's actually not a curtain; it's the northern lights. They happen in the northern parts of Planet Earth, and they are beautiful.

You know, God didn't have to make the sky so beautiful. I think He did it just so we would have something wonderful to enjoy. God loves beauty. He loves beauty in nature, and He smiles when He sees a beautiful, giving person. Will you be a beautiful giver today? Will you be one who shows by their cheerful soul that Jesus is a wonderful Savior? Tell a friend you love Jesus today and bring some beauty into their life.

Star Light, Star Bright

He who made the Pleiades and Orion, who turns blackness into dawn and darkens day into night, who calls for the waters of the sea and pours them out over the face of the land—the Lord is his name. Amos 5:8.

We're still watching the night sky on our nature hike today. It's so beautiful. Do you know what a constellation is? It's a group of stars in the sky that forms a picture. For instance, people long ago thought the constellation Orion, mentioned in today's verse, looked like a hunter with a sword hanging from his belt. There are many other constellations in the sky. If you find a book on the night sky, it will show the many pictures stars form.

Did you know you are like a constellation? The little things you do each day form a picture of who you are. If you say you love Jesus, they form a picture of Him too. What kind of constellation are your deeds forming today? Of course, we are all sinners. The only way we can form a good picture of Jesus is by sticking close to Him each day and doing what He's asked us to do. Let your deeds shine like little stars so others can see a constellation of Jesus shining in your life.

Very Fruity

Amos answered Amaziah, "I was neither a prophet
nor a prophet's son, but I was a shepherd, and I
also took care of sycamore-fig trees." Amos 7:14.

Imagine that. Here we are hiking through the fields of sycamore-fig trees and we find out that Amos, a prophet of God, was really just a shepherd and a farmer taking care of fruit trees. Isn't it amazing what God can do with a person who is willing to serve Him?

The sycamore tree of the Bible, even the one Zacchaeus climbed up, was a type of fig tree. Figs are a type of fruit that are full of seeds and very sweet. In order for them to grow properly, someone must take very good care of them. If they are taken care of by a skillful farmer, they will produce sweet, juicy fruit.

We're like fig trees. When we let Jesus take care of us, He will produce fruit for others to see. The Bible says you will know God's people by the fruit in their lives. In other words, people will see the love of Jesus shining through your actions. God can do amazing things with you and produce delicious fruit in your life. Let the Master Farmer take care of you today, and watch the sweet fruit grow.

24 AUGUST

Ripe and Ready

"What do you see, Amos?" he asked. "A basket of ripe fruit," I answered. Then the Lord said to me, "The time is ripe for my people Israel; I will spare them no longer." Amos 8:2.

Hike right over to that apple tree. Now, pick one of those apples. It looks a little green, but let's try one anyway. Oooh, that's sour! Apples sure do taste better when they're ripe, don't they? If you let them go too long, though, they'll turn brown and mushy. Yuck!

In today's verse God was saying His people were like a basket of ripe fruit. They were ripe, or ready to be punished, because they hadn't obeyed. God doesn't like to punish, but sometimes He must to teach us important lessons.

Being ripe and ready can be a good thing, too. It can mean you are mature. When a person is mature, it means they think about the things they do. They think about what will happen if they do them. They think about how to help others, and they think about growing closer to Jesus. God wants you to be ripe and ready. He wants you to be ready to learn what He wants to teach you. Ask God to ripen you for heaven today, and sweeten the lives of those around you.

246

A Flood of Blessings

The Lord, the Lord Almighty, he who touches the earth and it melts, and all who live in it mourn—the whole land rises like the Nile, then sinks like the river of Egypt. Amos 9:5.

Here we are hiking right next to the Nile River in Egypt. This is so cool! This is the same river we read about in the book of Exodus. When God sent the plagues, it turned to blood.

The Nile River has many animals living in and alongside it. There are big crocodiles, more than a dozen kinds of poisonous snakes, and insects that cause disease. It sounds pretty scary, doesn't it? The Nile River also used to flood every year in ancient times. It would bring up rich dirt from the river bottom, and farmers would use that good dirt to plant beautiful crops.

Sometimes life can be like the Nile. It can be dangerous. Sometimes bad things happen. But even though Satan may throw his poison at us and life seems to overflow with bad things, Jesus can make good things come from bad. He can bring rich soil into our lives and help us grow into the kind of people He wants us to be. So when bad things seem to poison you, look for Jesus to flood blessings into your life.

26 AUGUST

Swooping Sin

The pride of your heart has deceived you, you who live in the clefts of the rocks and make your home on the heights, you who say to yourself, "Who can bring me down to the ground?" Obadiah 1:3.

We're hiking right alongside a great cliff today. If you'll look straight up, you'll see tiny birds darting in and out of the cliffs. Now, if you'll look closely through your binoculars, you'll see little nests glued right to the cliff wall. Those birds are cliff swallows, and they live way up there all the time.

Today's verse talks about people who lived high in mountain caves. They thought they were safe; they thought no one could reach them there. You might think the cliff swallow is safe living high along the cliffs. It is safe from many things, but not from birds like hawks and eagles that look for smaller birds to eat.

If we are tempted to think we are safe living life on our own, we are mistaken. Only with Jesus in our life can we be safe from sin. If the cliff swallow stays in her nest along the wall, she'll be safe. We should stay in the safe nest of God's Word to keep us from temptation. That way sin won't swoop down and capture us.

High Riser

"You soar like the eagle and make your nest among the stars . . .," declares the Lord. Obadiah 1:4.

As we take our hike today, we're watching an eagle soar high into the sky. It seems to be circling and getting higher all at the same time. Is the eagle so light that it floats? Doesn't it obey the laws of gravity? Why do you think the eagle rises when it flies?

The answer is invisible. It's the air! That's right; it's warm air. We've already discovered the fact that warm air rises. When there is a column of warm air rising into the sky, the eagle just hops on and catches a ride. What great fun that must be!

When you have a smile on your face, people around you may wonder why you're so happy. When you stop to think, we have so much to be happy about. Jesus gave His life to save us. Right now He's building a mansion for us, and one day soon He'll come through the clouds and take us back to heaven with Him. That's a ton of things to be happy about. Hop on God's high rising column of joy today and soar with the happiness of knowing that the King of the universe loves you.

Gentle Giant

The Lord provided a great fish to swallow Jonah, and Jonah was inside the fish three days and three nights. Jonah 1:17.

Can you imagine being swallowed by a great fish? Now, the Bible doesn't say what kind of fish it was, but there are some fish in the ocean big enough to swallow a man. One of them is the whale shark.

Whale sharks can grow nearly 60 feet long. They are huge! As powerful as they are, though, they're very gentle. Humans have taken rides on their fins without making Mr. Whale Shark angry. As big and strong as these creatures are, whale sharks eat only small animals. In fact, most of the time the animals they eat are so small you and I can't even see them. If it was a whale shark that swallowed Jonah, maybe it threw him up because he was just too big.

God wants you to be strong and gentle like the whale shark. He wants you to be strong for Him and not easily offended when people hurt you, but He also wants you to be gentle. He wants you to look for ways you can help those who are hurting around you. He wants you always to show kindness. Be a whale shark today. Be a gentle giant!

Don't Be Wormy

At dawn the next day God provided a worm, which chewed the vine so that it withered. Jonah 4:7.

Poor Jonah. Let's hike right over to where he is and see why he's so upset. It seems he's preached to Nineveh and they accepted the God of heaven as their God. Why should he be so upset? Well, you see, Jonah thought those wicked people deserved to die. He thought God should have destroyed them. He spent three days in the belly of a fish and these people got forgiveness! Actually, all Jonah could think about was how angry he was. He wasn't thinking of anyone but himself.

Selfishness can be just like that little worm. It can eat away at us until we wither. We don't do anyone any good if we just focus on ourselves. God wants us to look out for others. He wants us to be happy when people change for the better. Jesus died so all of us can be in heaven—you, me, and those who do terrible things. Don't let selfishness eat away at you like that little worm ate the vine Jonah was sitting under. Live for Jesus today and show love to all those around you.

Water, I Need Water

When the sun rose, God provided a scorching east wind, and the sun blazed on Jonah's head so that he grew faint. He wanted to die, and said, "It would be better for me to die than to live." Jonah 4:8.

When God sent that scorching east wind on Jonah, with the sun blazing from above, Jonah wanted water so badly he thought he would die. Water. It's such a simple thing. Almost everywhere we've hiked this year we've found it. But think for a moment what would happen if you couldn't find it.

Well, you couldn't wash your clothes. You couldn't take a bath. You couldn't have a drink! Whoa, wait a minute. You could do without washing your clothes or taking a bath for a while (although no one would stand too close to you), but if you tried going without any drinking water for about four or five days, you would die. You simply cannot live without it.

You and I can't live without God either. He's our Savior. That means He keeps us from dying eternally. When He comes again, I want to live with Him forever, don't you? In order to live with Him we must be on His side. Place yourself on God's side today and drink deeply of the water of life.

Melting Mountains

The mountains melt beneath him and the valleys split apart, like wax before the fire, like water rushing down a slope. Micah 1:4.

Have you ever watched a birthday candle drip onto your cake as the fire melted it? You probably had to blow it out quickly before the top of your cake was completely covered by wax. Even though the flame was small, the wax dripped like water. It just couldn't stand the heat.

When today's verse says the "mountains melt beneath him and the valleys split apart, like wax before the fire," what do you think it means? Do you know who the "him" in the verse is? It's our heavenly Father. He sounds a bit scary, doesn't He?

What I've learned from this verse and others I've hiked through in God's Word is that our Father in heaven is someone to be respected. He's very powerful. But that's a good thing. I know He can take care of any problem I might have. I know He can protect me from Satan. I also know He loves me. I'm glad He can melt mountains like wax; it means I can trust Him to take good care of me.

1 SEPTEMBER

Ooh, That Hurts

Those who live in Maroth writhe in pain, waiting for relief, because disaster has come. Micah 1:12.

Ouch! Why do people say that word? It's because they've been hurt, of course. But do you know why people hurt? Do you wish the next time you pinched your finger that it wouldn't hurt? Well, it sounds like a good idea, but it's not!

Inside your body are little stringlike things called nerves. When you pinch your finger, or burn your hand, or hit your nose, you hit those nerves. Your nerves then send signals to let your brain know you've been hurt and you feel pain. Your brain will tell your finger or hand or other part of your body that it should move away from the pain. Actually, it's a good thing to feel pain, isn't it? If you didn't, you'd just keep your hand right on that hot stove.

Sometimes we must learn painful lessons in life too. Sometimes it's because we've done something wrong. Sometimes it's a mistake someone else has made. Many times it's not a part of our body that hurts; it's our feelings. The pain helps us learn not to do those things again. God wants us to learn from mistakes. We may feel pain sometimes, but how would we learn without it?

Food for Squid

You will again have compassion on us; you will tread our sins underfoot and hurl all our iniquities into the depths of the sea. Micah 7:19.

One of my dreams is to take off my hiking boots and ride in a submarine. But I don't want to ride in just any submarine. I want to ride in one of those little scientific bubble submarines so I can go deep, deep, deep into the ocean depths and look for giant squid. That's right, giant squid! They're huge creatures, with eight long arms and two tentacles that they use to catch their food and eat it. I sure wouldn't want to get in their way.

But what's that I see down here in the ocean? They're sins—big ones, little ones, sins of all kinds. How did they get down here? Read today's verse. God threw them down here. What that means is that God has forgiven you and me, and He's "thrown" our sins away so no one can find them. It means that when we ask for forgiveness, we don't have to worry about our sins anymore. They're as gone as if a giant squid had eaten them. No one can ever bring them back. I wonder what the favorite food of giant squid might be. I wonder . . .

Get Out of the Storm

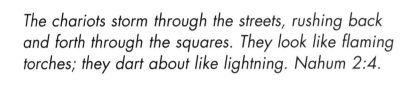

The chariots storm through the streets, rushing back and forth through the squares. They look like flaming torches; they dart about like lightning. Nahum 2:4.

Run! It's starting to storm. Look at those angry clouds. It's beginning to rain. *Crrrack!* Did you see that flash of lightning and hear that clap of thunder? Lightning sure is powerful and dangerous, and we need to protect ourselves. Do you know what to do to protect yourself from lightning? There are several things you can do, but one of the most important is this: If you are outside and there's lightning, get inside as quickly as possible. It's important to get out of the water, get dry, and be protected. Don't stay where the lightning is!

God is our protector in a world filled with the lightning darts Satan throws at us. Some people think they don't need God's protection. They believe they are tough enough to stand against Satan's attacks, but don't you believe it. Satan is a tough enemy. We need to run to God's protection and get out of the storm. Go where it's safe. Don't stay where the lightning is. Run to God's house. You'll be safe there.

Multiply Your Happiness

Multiply like grasshoppers, multiply like locusts! Nahum 3:15.

Multiply, multiply, multiply. Are we talking about math here? No way, we're talking about grasshoppers and locusts. Today we're hiking through a field filled with them. Pretty soon this field may not even be here. These creatures can eat a field "gone" in no time.

Grasshoppers can multiply, or make new grasshoppers, at an amazing rate. Mother grasshoppers can lay more than 2,000 eggs in a season. If every mama grasshopper laid 2,000 eggs and they all hatched, there would be millions upon millions. That's a lot of baby grasshoppers. It's no wonder there's so many of these creatures.

Lies can be like grasshoppers. Once a person begins to tell lies, they often multiply. Some people tell so many lies, they don't know when they're telling the truth and when they're lying. And just as grasshoppers can eat a field "gone," lies can eat away our happiness. Those who tell lies may think they're smart, but they're actually hurting themselves. Do yourself a favor—tell the truth and multiply your happiness.

No One to Help

Nothing can heal your wound; your injury is fatal. Everyone who hears the news about you claps his hands at your fall, for who has not felt your endless cruelty? Nahum 3:19.

If you were hiking along a trail and found someone who had fallen and was bleeding, what would you do? The very first thing you must do is to stop the bleeding. You should use a cloth and wear gloves if you have them, and press down on the bleeding wound. It's important to keep a person from losing too much blood. You would be a "good Samaritan" for helping the person.

Today's verse, though, tells a sad story. It talks about someone no one wants to help. In fact, people are clapping when this person falls and hurts themself. Why aren't others sad? It's because the injured person is a cruel person. That person hasn't treated people nicely at all, and now no one wants to help.

Remember that a "good Samaritan" should always help anyone they can, even a cruel person. But there's another very important lesson to learn here. Be a nice person. Treat others like you want to be treated. Help others when they're in trouble. Someday when you're in trouble, you might find someone happy to help you.

Runnin' Wolves

Their horses are swifter than leopards, fiercer than wolves at dusk. Their cavalry gallops headlong; their horsemen come from afar. They fly like a vulture swooping to devour. Habakkuk 1:8.

Careful now. We're hiking in the land of wolves. They hunt around here when the sun goes down. We're a little too big for them to eat, but we don't want to get in their way. Wolves travel and hunt in packs or groups of up to 40. That's a lot of wolves all in one place.

In Matthew 7:15 Jesus said, "Watch out for false prophets. They come to you in sheep's clothing, but inwardly they are ferocious wolves." Sadly, what Jesus meant was that some people teach the wrong things about God. He called them "ferocious wolves." But you and I don't have to be afraid of the wolves. We can protect ourselves against them by learning from God's Word each day. The Bible verses we learn help us know the truth about God. They help us know when someone is telling us the wrong things about our Father in heaven. Learn as much as you can from the Bible and make the wolves "turn tail" and run.

Swimming in the Right Direction

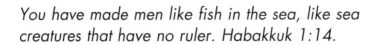

You have made men like fish in the sea, like sea creatures that have no ruler. Habakkuk 1:14.

Today we'll take off our hiking boots and put on our flippers. We'll be swimming in the ocean so we can see all of the beautiful fish God has made. There are so many, they're so colorful, and they're so smart. We know they're smart because so many of them go to school. Well, sort of. What I mean is that many fish travel in schools. Are you laughing? What . . . you didn't think that was funny? Oh, well.

Some fish travel in schools—groups of thousands upon thousands. Today's verse says the fish have no ruler. It sure looks like that when they travel in schools. They all just seem to follow the crowd, going wherever everyone else goes.

We have to be careful of the crowd we travel with. We have to make sure that the group we're hanging with is going in the right direction and traveling in the right way. Be smart. Make sure the "school" you're swimming with is sailing in the right direction.

Tough Feet

The Sovereign Lord is my strength; he makes my feet like the feet of a deer, he enables me to go on the heights. Habakkuk 3:19.

You know, sometimes all this hiking is hard, isn't it? Our feet get sore, our muscles ache, and it's hard to climb up the mountains. I wish I could climb as easily as the mule deer. If you look in the right place at the right time in the Rocky Mountains of the western United States and Canada, you will see a large deer called the mule deer. The mule deer can climb and even run up the rocks and mountains that are so hard for humans to climb. They can do it easily because God has created them with a special kind of hoof that is flexible and tough all at the same time.

God can make you flexible and tough all at the same time, too. Sometimes things happen to us that are as hard as climbing up a mountain. But God can strengthen you and give you "tough feet" like He gives the mule deer. He'll help you to bend, but not break. He'll help you climb up life's tough trails and keep you strong on your way to the mountains of heaven.

Number One

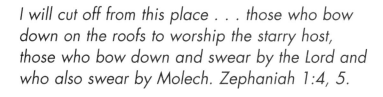

*I will cut off from this place . . . those who bow
down on the roofs to worship the starry host,
those who bow down and swear by the Lord and
who also swear by Molech. Zephaniah 1:4, 5.*

Today (or should I say tonight?) we're on a night hike.
We're way up on a mountaintop away from the lights of
the city. It's because we want to see some other lights. In fact,
there are hundreds of billions of them. We're looking at the
Milky Way Galaxy. The Milky Way is a band of stars you can
see stretching across the night sky. Our sun is part of it.
Imagine—billions and billions of our suns. That's an amazing
galaxy! What's even more amazing is that there are millions of
other galaxies beyond the Milky Way. Our God sure is a wonderful Creator.

If you'll look at today's verse, you'll read a sad story. It's a
story about some people who were so amazed by the Milky
Way and all the other stars in the sky that they worshiped them
instead of the God who created them. God must have been
sad. He created those stars for us and, sadly, some people worship His creation instead of Him. Don't let anything take the
place of God in your life. He wants to be your number one!

262

Trippin' Down the Dusty Trail

They will walk like blind men, because they have sinned against the Lord. Their blood will be poured out like dust and their entrails. . . . Zephaniah 1:17.

Hiking like blind men—that would be tough, wouldn't it? That's what the people in today's verse were doing. Sadly, Zephaniah was talking about God's people. They didn't just make a simple mistake or two. They had said to God, "We don't want You anymore—we want to worship other gods." How sad God must have been and how lost they were.

I want you to look at the last word in the verse above, "entrails." Do you know what those are? No, they are not the trails the blind men were walking on. Entrails are intestines. Your intestines are made up of a long tube in your body that helps you digest the food and water you put into your stomach. God made this special path for your food to travel. He's also made a special path in life for you to travel. Stay on God's path. Keep worshiping Him today. Let Him guide you. Don't get lost like a blind man on a dusty trail.

Opinion Number One

Surely Moab will become like Sodom, the Ammonites like Gomorrah—a place of weeds and salt pits. Zephaniah 2:9.

Weeds. Everywhere we hike you can see them. We've talked about poisonous weeds before, but today we're going to talk about a much more common type of weed. In fact, you probably have them growing in your front yard.

I'm talking about dandelions. Most people dig them out or cut them out of their yard. No one I know likes to have them in their lawn. But there are some farmers in New Jersey that like them. They like them because they earn hundreds of thousands of dollars with dandelions. You see, some people eat them. And these farmers sell them to those people. It's true; some people eat the green leaves of dandelions. They really do have lots of vitamins. Who would have ever thought some people would eat what other people throw away?

People like and value many different things. People have lots of different opinions. Make sure you know what God wants you to like and think. Read His Word daily. His opinion is the one that really counts.

My, What Big Ears You Have

Flocks and herds will lie down there, creatures of every kind. The desert owl and the screech owl will roost on her columns. Their calls will echo through the windows, rubble will be in the doorways, the beams of cedar will be exposed. Zephaniah 2:14.

Quiet now, we're on another night hike and we don't want to miss seeing the screech owl. The screech owl is a small owl with big ears. He can fly almost silently, sneak up on a big old rat, and catch it. How does he find the rat in the dark? Well, for one thing, Mr. Screech Owl has very sharp eyes. He can see in almost complete darkness. The other thing old "Screech" has is big ears. He listens very carefully for movement in the grass.

You and I could be a little more like the screech owl sometimes. We could have bigger ears that are willing to listen carefully to other people—our parents, our friends, and our teachers. We could open our eyes a little wider to see those who are hurting and help them in some way. There are many lessons we can learn from Mr. Screech Owl. Grow some big eyes and ears today and be a helper.

13 SEPTEMBER

Blight or Light

"I struck all the work of your hands with blight, mildew and hail, yet you did not turn to me," declares the Lord. Haggai 2:17.

Today we're hiking through an apple orchard. Don't you just love the smell of fresh apples hanging from the trees and weighing the branches down? I love the shiny red color . . . wait, what's that? Look at that ugly, bumpy-looking stuff on those apples over there. And look, there's more over there. It's what's called "blight" in today's verse.

This blight is called fire blight. Fire blight is a disease that eats away at pear and apple trees. Bacteria cause it. Bacteria are tiny organisms so small you can't see them. But how do the bacteria get to the pears and apples? You'll never believe it. When the wind blows and the rain comes down, the bacteria "fly" from tree to tree.

There's something else that hurts people that bad and gets spread from person to person. It's gossip. Gossip is talking about other people when it isn't our business. It's passing around rumors that hurt other people. We shouldn't hurt others by passing around hurtful things. Don't let your words be a blight today; let them be filled with light and help others to see Jesus more clearly.

266

Trained for Eternity

14 SEPTEMBER

Before that time there were no wages for man or beast. Zechariah 8:10.

Today we've hiked right into the middle of the three rings. What are the three rings? I'm talking about the circus, of course. Have you ever heard of a three-ring circus? We're here because today's verse is talking about wages for a beast. There are animals working here, aren't there? What about those elephants and the monkeys and tigers? Shouldn't they get paid? Of course, all the animals want is a good meal. They don't even have bank accounts. Their human owners and trainers are the ones that get paid.

Did you know that you're being trained? Not like an animal, of course. God made you with the ability to think and feel many more things than a monkey. You're being trained to be an honest, trustworthy boy or girl who loves Jesus. That's why you're reading this book. Did you know that? And all the payment your parents, teachers, and other adults want is for you to be a follower of Jesus and to be with you in heaven someday. Take your training seriously. Don't worry about being paid in money. Jesus has paid the price of heaven for you!

267

15 SEPTEMBER

Christmastime in September

Wail, O pine tree, for the cedar has fallen; the stately trees are ruined! Wail, oaks of Bashan; the dense forest has been cut down! Zechariah 11:2.

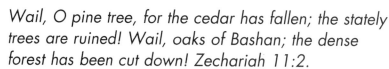

Are you ready for Christmas? Now, I know it's more than three months away, but don't you just love to think about it anytime during the year? Lots of things come to mind when I think of Christmas: Jesus coming to this earth, family and friends, presents and Christmas trees. Most Christmas trees are some kind of pine tree, like the pine mentioned in today's verse. Christmas trees are pretty, but I think I like them most for their scent. A Christmas tree makes the whole house smell delicious.

Today, why don't you be a Christmas tree Christian? That's right. You can make a whole room smell better. Not by wearing perfume, but by being a kind and loving person. By being a loving and lovable Christian, you can fill a whole day with the beautiful fragrance of Jesus.

Today you may meet up with some people who aren't very happy. You might be tempted to be unhappy right back at them. Don't do it! Let the sweet-smelling love of Jesus come from your heart, and watch it become Christmastime in September.

The Beautiful Life-giver

On that day there will be no light, no cold or frost. Zechariah 14:6.

Today we're hiking in the very early morning. Do you hear that *crunch, crunch, crunch* under our feet? Do you know what that is? No, we're not stepping on candy or pencils or cereal. We're walking on frost. It's all over the ground, and when the sun comes up, you'll see how beautiful it is. When the sunlight reflects off the tiny ice crystals, it's so pretty.

Do you know where frost comes from? The air all around us is filled with tiny droplets of water. In parts of the world where it gets cold at night and the temperature falls to freezing, those water droplets will freeze and fall to the ground forming beautiful ice crystals all around.

While those ice crystals are beautiful, farmers don't like them much. They can kill plants. How can something so beautiful be so destructive? That's the way sin is. Satan makes sin look like a very good idea, but it only leads to trouble and finally death. Follow the only beautiful thing that can bring life—eternal life. That thing is, of course, a person—it's Jesus! He's the beautiful life-giver.

Don't Wrestle . . . Nestle!

This is the plague with which the Lord will strike all the nations that fought against Jerusalem . . . their eyes . . . in their sockets. Zechariah 14:12.

Eyes in their sockets—that's a pretty amazing thing! If we could become tiny hikers, climb right up on somebody's nose, and look into their eyes, we would see an amazing thing. Yes, we'd see eyeballs and those are very amazing, but we'd also see where those eyeballs sit. They sit in sockets.

Your skull is made of eight bones that fit together perfectly to form a protective container for your brain. Your brain is soft and needs protection. But your eyeballs are soft, and they need protection too. The only problem is that they're on the outside of your head. So what did God, our wonderful Creator, do to protect them? He nestled them inside bone sockets, or holes that protect them on all sides but one. Then He made bones that stick out farther than your eyes, all around the front of your eyeballs. That's an amazing design!

God knows just how to protect you and me too. Even when we can't figure out how to protect ourselves, He always has a way. Run to Jesus, your protector, and nestle in His mighty arms of love.

only the Best

I have turned his mountains into a wasteland and left his inheritance to the desert jackals. Malachi 1:3.

Quiet now. Shhh. . . . We're on the trail of the desert jackal. Now, you should be afraid of the wolflike jackal. But we need to be more afraid of the lion. That's right! Here's how it works. The lion hunts down an animal and eats what it wants. Then the jackal comes in behind and picks up the scraps. The jackal will eat anything. It's a scavenger.

Now, it might be OK for the jackal to be a scavenger, but don't you be one. A scavenger feeds on whatever leftovers and garbage it can find. I'm not talking about eating from the garbage can. What I mean is that you shouldn't put garbage into your head. You and I should read the very best books, watch the kind of TV that can help us learn, and look at the very best magazines. In other words, don't put garbage in your mind the way the jackal puts garbage in its stomach.

Fill your brain with the kind of things that will help you grow closer to Jesus. I suppose the jackal has to be a scavenger to survive. You don't. Look for only the best—that's what Jesus wants for you.

Sticking Up Your Nose

"And you say, 'What a burden!' and you sniff at it contemptuously," says the Lord Almighty. Malachi 1:13.

Sniff, sniff, sniff! Most of the time I like what I sniff, but not always. One of the worst smells I've ever sniffed is a skunk. Wow, they stink! I used to live in the country where many skunks lived. As I hiked down the steps of my back porch one day, I placed my foot too close to the edge of the porch. Down I went into the woodpile sitting next to the house.

Of course, I hurt myself, but I soon didn't even notice my bumps and bruises, because I was staring right at the wrong end of a skunk! My first reaction was to stick my nose in the air. I didn't want it anywhere near that skunk. Unfortunately, I couldn't stick my nose far enough into the air. *Pshhhhh!* Skunk spray was everywhere—and most of it was on me!

Today's verse talks about people who "stick up their noses." The sad thing was that they were sticking their noses up at God. How sad and disobedient. Obey God with a joyful heart. Gladly do the things He's asked you to do. You'll be so much happier, and you'll find that He makes life smell sweet.

Pest Control

"I will prevent pests from devouring your crops, and the vines in your fields will not cast their fruit," says the Lord Almighty. Malachi 3:11.

Today we march our hiking boots right through a farmer's field. Just look at all the beautiful stalks of corn, and the beets over in that field. They're such a pretty green. But a beautiful field of vegetables today can soon be a brown, withered, dead piece of land—and all because of a little pest called the aphid.

Aphids are tiny, tiny insects you'll find on the underside of plant leaves. They have hard little beaks they use to punch holes in the leaf and suck out the juices. Some aphids even inject poison into the leaf, which makes it shrivel up, die, and fall off. But the aphid has a natural enemy. The ladybug is feared among aphids. Ladybugs can fly in and eat aphids by the hundreds of thousands.

Our verse today says that God can even protect our crops from being eaten by pests like the aphid. But He's more powerful than a ladybug. If God is interested in even the farmer's crops, you know He's interested in all the things in your life, too. So go ahead; give Him a chance to take care of the pests in your life.

Indestructible

Store up for yourselves treasures in heaven, where moth and rust do not destroy, and where thieves do not break in and steal. Matthew 6:20.

We're on another night hike. It's a special night because it's our first night hiking in the New Testament of the Bible.

Today we're looking for something very special and very beautiful. We're looking for moths. Many moths like to fly around bright lights. Look over there. Some of them are so big and so pretty. But as lovely as moths can be, they can also be very destructive.

Moths often lay their eggs on wool coats and sweaters in the closets of humans. When the eggs hatch, the little caterpillars that will soon become moths begin to eat big holes in those expensive clothes.

In our verse for today, Jesus tells us not to put too much value in our clothes or houses or other treasures. He knows something as tiny as a moth's caterpillar can destroy them. You and I should put our trust in Jesus and our treasure in heaven. No one can take His love from us, and no one can destroy the mansions He's preparing. They're indestructible.

Pure as Lilies

And why do you worry about clothes? See how the lilies of the field grow. They do not labor or spin. Matthew 6:28.

One of my favorite places to hike is in an art museum. I love to look at the pictures that artists have thought of and painted. One of the most amazing museums I've ever been to is in Paris, France. It's called the Louvre. I remember seeing a painting in the Louvre of the angel Gabriel coming to visit Mary, to tell her the good news that she was going to be the mother of Jesus. In Gabriel's hand were lilies. Lilies are such beautiful white flowers. The artist used lilies because they have come to mean purity, and there's nothing purer than Jesus.

Jesus wants us to be pure also. Sometimes we do things we shouldn't, and we worry that we could ever become a pure, honest boy or girl. Jesus doesn't want us to worry. Our job is to talk with Him every day, read His Word, and think about Him as much as we can; His job is to make us pure. He doesn't want us to worry, because He knows we can't make ourselves pure. Get in touch with Jesus today. He's the only one who can make you and me as pure as lilies.

Get Out of the Mud

Do not give dogs what is sacred; do not throw your pearls to pigs. If you do, they may trample them under their feet, and then turn and tear you to pieces. Matthew 7:6.

Pigs. Whoa, can they be stinky. There's a pig farm next to a highway not too far from my house that I can smell when I drive by. I can smell those pigs even with the windows closed and the air-conditioner on. They roll around in the mud all day and seem to be having a good time, but I don't think they can smell themselves, or they'd want a bath quick. Some people have pet pigs. I've even seen pigs dressed up in little pig clothes, but can you imagine giving some of your best clothes or precious things to a stinky old pig?

What did Jesus mean when He said not to "throw your pearls to pigs"? He meant that, sadly, not everyone wants to hear us talk about our Father in heaven. Some people want to roll around in sin.

Jesus loves even those who want to stay in sin. So even if you can't tell them about Jesus today, let them see Him by the way you live your life. Maybe one day they'll get out of the mud.

I Am Willing

Jesus reached out his hand and touched the man. "I am willing," he said. "Be clean!" Immediately he was cured of his leprosy. Matthew 8:3.

Today I'd like for us to imagine we're hiking in the land of the Bible thousands of years ago. We're hiking through a lonely, cave-filled part of the country. I hear some groaning, as if someone is hurting. Listen, it's coming from inside that cave. Let's look to see if we can help. Oh, that poor man. His hands and feet are all wrapped up; and his nose—what's wrong with his nose, and what are those white blotches all over his face? It's leprosy.

Leprosy is caused by little bacteria that eat away at a person's skin. It's very sad, but in Bible times there was no medicine that doctors could give people with leprosy. People who had it were sent away to live in caves away from everyone else. Eventually they died in the caves.

Like today's verse says, Jesus could heal even leprosy. Today He can heal you, too. It's true, He can heal disease; but more important, He can clean the sin from your life. Won't you tell Him today that you too are willing to be clean?

25
SEPTEMBER

Prayer Cords

"Lord," he said, "my servant lies at home paralyzed and in terrible suffering." Matthew 8:6.

We've been hiking together for quite a while, haven't we? Most people get very tired after hiking for a long time. But think how happy we can be about getting tired while we're hiking. What? You don't understand? Many people can't walk at all. Like the servant in today's verse, many people are paralyzed and can't even move. This often happens when people have a spinal cord injury.

Your spinal cord runs down your backbone and carries all the nerves and information your body needs to work, including the information you need to walk. If your spinal cord is cut or badly injured, you may not be able to walk at all.

Prayer can be like a spinal cord of information and love from our Father in heaven. By talking with Him each day in prayer we can receive everything we need to live our lives for Him. Don't do anything to injure your connection with Jesus. He loves you and wants to help you walk for Him each day. And that's something you can do, even if you find yourself in a wheelchair.

Be Still

When the demon was driven out, the man who had been mute spoke. The crowd was amazed and said, "Nothing like this has ever been seen in Israel." Matthew 9:33.

We've been hiking a long way now. We're getting close to the end of September. I've enjoyed our little talks each day. I hope you have. Of course, we're "talking" through words printed on a page. If we were really hiking next to each other, we'd probably be using our voices to speak. But think about what it would be like if you couldn't speak at all. You try, but nothing comes out of your mouth—like the man in today's verse, you are mute.

Not being able to speak would be difficult for most of us who are used to speaking. We would have to learn to communicate some other way. The truth is, sometimes we talk too much anyway. The Bible tells us, "Be still, and know that I am God" (Psalm 46:10). Sometimes we just need to stop talking, quiet everything around us, and let God speak in the stillness. Take some time today to be mute. While you're being quiet, listen for God to give you thoughts of Him and learn to know God better.

Something to Chirp About

Don't be afraid; you are worth more than many sparrows. Matthew 10:31.

One of the things I've enjoyed most on our hikes is the chirping of the birds. They're all around us, and they make things so cheery. We've seen many kinds of birds, but we've seen more sparrows than any other kind. They seem to be all over. Jesus talked about sparrows more than once. Just two verses before today's verse, in Matthew 10:29, Jesus said He cared if even one of them fell to the ground. Even though some people don't care too much for sparrows because there's so many of them, Jesus cares for every one.

Today's verse tells us that we "are worth more than many sparrows." God loves us so much. He made us like Himself. He made us to worship and to love Him. We really are His favorites. When you're in trouble, when you've made mistakes, when it seems that everyone is against you and you're feeling quite sad, remember this—you are worth more than tons of birds to the Creator of the universe. Now, that's something to chirp about!

Don't Get Squirrelly With Me

As he was scattering the seed, some fell along the path, and the birds came and ate it up. Matthew 13:4.

If you were to hike into my backyard, you would see a bird feeder hanging on the back porch. It's filled with seeds for birds to eat. As in today's verse, seeds are one of the favorite foods of many birds. But it's not just birds that like seeds.

I have so many squirrels in my yard. They're a bit pesky at times. They jump from the big trees in the backyard and onto my roof. Then they carefully walk onto the pole that holds my bird feeder away from the house. Like a tightrope walker, they balance their way out to the bird feeder. Then they hang upside down and steal the seeds I put there for the birds.

Satan wants to steal from you too. He wants to steal your "God-time" away from you. He wants to keep you so busy with life that you have no time for God. Don't let him do it. Don't let Satan get squirrelly with you. Tell him you're going to spend time with God each day no matter what it takes.

The Little Things

This people's heart has become callused; they hardly hear with their ears, and they have closed their eyes. Matthew 13:15.

Have you ever tried to hike with your eyes closed? It's not a good idea, is it? It's an especially bad idea if you're hiking on a mountain trail. When you close your eyes, what do you see? Do you see anything? Do you see light? What you really see is the inside of your eyelids. Your eyelids are pretty amazing. They close out the light when you want to sleep. They help wash water over your eyeballs to rinse the dust away. They even protect your sensitive eyeballs if something is about to land on them.

God thought of everything, didn't He? If you or I had been the creator, we might have been so excited about making an eyeball that we would have forgotten about the eyelid to cover it up. It shows me that God really is concerned with the little things.

God wants us to get rid of the little things in our lives that keep us from loving Him fully, and He wants to take care of the little things in our lives that need taking care of. As you can see, our God is a big God, but He also cares about the little things.

Keep Looking Up

He replied, "When evening comes, you say, 'It will be fair weather, for the sky is red,' and in the morning, 'Today it will be stormy, for the sky is red and overcast.' You know how to interpret the appearance of the sky, but you cannot interpret the signs of the times." Matthew 16:2, 3.

Did you know you can tell the weather by looking at the sky? Well, of course you did. If it's a cloudy sky, you know it might rain. But did you know that if the sky is red in the evening, it will probably be a sunny sky the next day?

Do you think Jesus was just trying to be a weather forecaster in today's verse? I don't think so. He was talking to some of the church leaders. He was telling them that even though they could tell the weather by looking at the sky, they couldn't see that He was the Savior of the world. They just couldn't see the signs that pointed to Him.

Today there are more signs of the times. The Bible says when there are wars and rumors of wars, earthquakes, and bad things happening in our world, we can know that Jesus is coming again very soon. Keep looking up—one day soon you'll see more than the weather.

Usin' Things and Lovin' People

Woe to you, teachers of the law and Pharisees, you hypocrites! You give a tenth of your spices—mint, dill and cummin. But you have neglected the more important matters of the law—justice, mercy and faithfulness. You should have practiced the latter, without neglecting the former. Matthew 23:23.

Smell the delicious flavor of all those mint plants. Today we're hiking right through an herb garden. Herb, the herb farmer, has planted all kinds of mint: spearmint, peppermint, horsemint, wild mint, and many others. Most people use mint for food, but some people many years ago used mint for money. That's right. The Pharisees used mint to pay their tithe at church. They were so careful to do everything right that they even tithed their garden!

Now, there's nothing wrong with being careful to do the right thing. God wants us to do that. But here's the problem the Pharisees had. They forgot the other really important stuff like loving people and treating them fairly. No one really cared that they were so careful tithing. They were downright mean sometimes, and that doesn't lead anyone to God. Be careful to do the right things, but don't forget what's really important—usin' things and lovin' people, and not the other way around.

Bugs Away

You blind guides! You strain out a gnat but swallow a camel. Matthew 23:24.

Slap! Swat! Have you ever had to do that on a hike? Have you ever had to shoo away the mosquitoes and flies and gnats? I have, and it's no fun. I just don't like it when those little critters are bugging me while I'm trying to have a nice hike. They can really spoil things. If you let them bother you too much, they're all you think about.

"Gnat" is really a word for many different kinds of small two-winged insects. One kind of gnat, called the buffalo gnat, can drive a full-grown horse crazy. Can you believe something so small can be so pesky?

What do you think Jesus was talking about in today's verse? Actually, He was talking about the same thing He was talking to the church leaders about in yesterday's verse. They were so worried about little unimportant things, and weren't worried enough about the really big things—like loving people. So today let's find someone to love and really show them we care. Do something special for someone. Don't worry about the little things that bug you about that person. Love them the way Jesus does and ask Him to take the bugs away.

3
OCTOBER

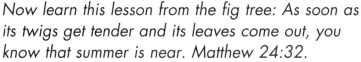

Summer's Coming

Now learn this lesson from the fig tree: As soon as its twigs get tender and its leaves come out, you know that summer is near. Matthew 24:32.

Can you tell by looking at the trees when summer is coming? Well, of course you can. You've been paying attention as we've hiked through the Bible, haven't you? You can tell that summer is coming when little green buds begin to break out all over the tree branches. Those buds are the very beginnings of leaves. If this was spring, they'd be bursting out green as can be in just a few weeks.

Jesus was teaching His followers a lesson in today's verse. He said that just as you can tell when summer is coming by looking at the tree branches, you can also tell when He will be coming again by the signs He told us about in Matthew 24.

Don't you want Jesus to come again soon? Won't it be so much fun to spend the rest of eternity with Him in heaven? He's our best friend, and He can hardly wait to see us. When you see the buds breaking out of the tree branches, remember this: Jesus is coming again soon, and He can't wait to break out of the clouds and take you home with Him.

Making God's Day

A woman came to him with an alabaster jar of very expensive perfume, which she poured on his head as he was reclining at the table. Matthew 26:7.

Today we're taking a break from our hike. I want you to imagine you are at the dinner table with Jesus in today's verse. We're at the house of Simon—a very wealthy and respected man. But who's that coming through the door? It's a woman, and she's taking a very expensive perfume from a very expensive jar and pouring it on Jesus' head. Why is she doing that? In Bible times that was usually done only after a person had died, to help the body smell good.

Maybe this woman knew that Jesus would soon die, but she didn't want to wait until He was dead to do something special for Him. She wanted Him to know how much she loved Him right then.

Why don't you let Jesus know how much you love Him today? Let Him know He is the most important person in the universe to you. Let Him know right now. It's the very best time. Jesus deserves our very best, doesn't He? Tell Him today that you love Him. It's a simple way to make His day.

Behind the Thorns

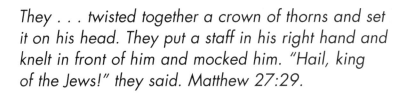

They . . . twisted together a crown of thorns and set it on his head. They put a staff in his right hand and knelt in front of him and mocked him. "Hail, king of the Jews!" they said. Matthew 27:29.

There's a beautiful river I like to visit. My two boys, Christopher and Michael, like to go with me when I hike there. I think they like the river too, but what they like most of all is catching lizards. There are hundreds of lizards there. The lizards like to crawl over and around the many boulders—and they are fast! Being fast makes them hard to catch, but what makes it even harder is where they hide. They hide in plain sight behind the thorns. You see, around most of the rocks are prickly thorns. If something tries to attack, the lizards run behind the thorns for protection.

Jesus was behind the thorns that soldiers put on His head many years ago. And just like the thorns protect the lizards at the river, the thorns on Jesus are for protection too. They didn't protect Jesus, though; they protected us. Because Jesus wore them for us, we have protection from sin. I love Him so much, don't you? Let Him know today that you're glad He hid behind the thorns in plain sight.

Never Thirsty

He was in the desert forty days, being tempted by Satan. He was with the wild animals, and angels attended him. Mark 1:13.

Have you ever hiked through a desert? I've driven through a desert in the summer. It was so hot and dry! There weren't many trees, and there weren't many lakes. In fact, there was hardly any water anywhere in that desert. That's why deserts are called deserts, you know.

Jesus must have been very weak and thirsty during those 40 days in the desert. Today's verse also tells us that during Jesus' time in the desert, Satan was tempting Him. It must have been very difficult for Jesus to say no to Satan when He was so thirsty for water.

You see, even though Jesus was thirsty for the kind of water that runs from your faucet, most of all, He wanted the "water of life." Revelation 22:1 says the water of life comes from the river of life in heaven. Jesus was looking forward to heaven and spending time with His Father, and someday with you and me. Don't give in to sin for things that don't last. Make sure you're searching for the water of life—drink some today, and keep hiking to heaven.

7
OCTOBER

Deep Roots

When the sun came up, the plants were scorched, and they withered because they had no root. Mark 4:6.

Have you ever hiked through the woods and tripped on a big tree root that stretched across the trail? It's amazing how big tree roots can get. They grow deep into the ground and soak up water and plant food. If those big roots weren't soaking up all that good stuff, those big trees wouldn't be so big.

Today's verse tells us that some plants die when the hot sun comes out because they have no roots. What Jesus meant was that many people who want to be Christians don't stay Christians for very long, because they aren't "rooting" themselves in Jesus; they aren't digging their "Christian" roots deep into the Bible.

It's so important that each day we get to know Jesus as our friend. Plant yourself in God's love while the weather is good. He'll give you all the water of life and plant food you need to grow strong in Him. Grow in Jesus now, and you'll stay strong even when Satan heats things up with temptation.

Stopping Storms

A furious squall came up, and the waves broke over the boat, so that it was nearly swamped. Mark 4:37.

There's a true story about a group of boys that went to school in a very unusual place. Where? you ask. Well, they went to school on a sailboat. They traveled on the ocean while learning math, science, reading, and sailing. One day they were met face to face with a squall. A squall is a very sudden storm with strong winds and dropping temperatures. The sad ending to that story was that the boat sank and everyone on board died.

In today's verse the disciples thought they might drown. They came face to face with a squall too. The wind picked up and the temperature dropped. The disciples were very afraid. They screamed to Jesus, who was sleeping in the back of the boat. They begged Him to help. He simply stood up and told the wind to stop—and it did! Amazing!

Sometimes I get worried about things that happen. You might do that sometimes too. Remember this—if Jesus can stop a storm, He can solve your problems. Call on Him and let Him calm your squall.

9 OCTOBER

Green and Full of Energy

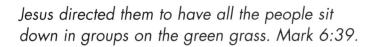

Jesus directed them to have all the people sit down in groups on the green grass. Mark 6:39.

They hiked up onto the hill. Jesus invited them all to sit down on the green grass. I'm sure it was a beautiful day.

It's so nice to sit down in green grass in the summertime, isn't it? Did you ever wonder why the grass is green—why it leaves such stains on your pants when you slide on it? It's all because of chlorophyll.

Chlorophyll is a chemical found in the cells of plants that turns sunlight into energy. That's an amazing thing, isn't it? God gave grass the ability to sit in the sun, soak up the light, and turn that light into plant food. What an amazing God we have!

God can give us all the spiritual food we need when we soak up His light and love. He can give us the energy to do the right thing, to help those around us, and to tell others about Jesus' love for them.

God is such a wonderful energy giver. He gives plants all they need to grow, and He gives us all we need to grow into energetic boys and girls living for Him.

Sticky Water

*When they saw him walking on the lake,
they thought he was a ghost. Mark 6:49.*

Walking on a lake. That's one place I've never tried to hike. Even though you and I could never walk on water, I know someone—or should I say "somebug"—that can. They're called water skimmers, and they zip right along the top of the water. How do they do it? It's called water tension.

Little parts of water called molecules want to stick together on the surface of the water. That's what the water skimmer rides on. Of course, you and I are much too heavy to hike on the top of a lake. Even though the water molecules want to stick together, we break through them anyway.

When Jesus walked on the water that day, He wasn't using the surface tension of the lake. He performed a miracle. He's the one who made the water, and His Father in heaven gave Him the power to break the rules of nature.

What a mighty God we serve. Did you know He can still perform miracles today? He can make the impossible happen. It might not be what we expect, but be sure of this—He's holding you up, and He won't let you drown.

11 OCTOBER

Spitting Our Blessings

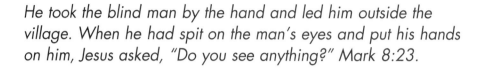

He took the blind man by the hand and led him outside the village. When he had spit on the man's eyes and put his hands on him, Jesus asked, "Do you see anything?" Mark 8:23.

Today's verse says Jesus hiked a blind man outside a village and then spit in his eyes. That doesn't seem to be a very nice thing to do, does it? In fact, it seems like a mean thing to do. But Jesus knew what He was doing. If you read the verses after Mark 8:23, you'll find that after Jesus spit in the man's eyes he could see!

Spit is another word for saliva. Saliva helps you digest your food. When you chew your food very carefully and mix it with the saliva in your mouth, it helps your stomach do its work better. Your saliva actually changes some of your food into other chemicals so you can get your vitamins. Isn't it amazing what a little spit can do?

Sometimes others may do mean things to you, but Jesus can turn what looks like a mean thing into something very good. He can turn curses into blessings. Remember this: If a little spit can help you digest your food and make a blind man see, it won't take much for Jesus to turn bad things into good for you.

A Sappy Story

Now learn this lesson from the fig tree: As soon as its twigs get tender and its leaves come out, you know that summer is near. Mark 13:28.

Don't you just love hiking through the woods in the spring? Do you remember doing that several months ago? It can be a little muddy, but I just love to see new life coming into the trees. The branches are so tender and sweet-smelling. The reason they smell that way is that they are full of fresh sap that's being pushed up from the roots and into the branches. This helps the tree grow strong and healthy.

Jesus said in today's verse that when you see the twigs get tender you'll know it's spring and that summer is coming soon. If you read on in Mark 13, you'll find out that Jesus was talking about His second coming. He said there will be clues so we'll know when He is about to come again.

I'm so glad that Jesus is coming again. I can't wait to see His big smile when He breaks through the clouds to come and take us home to heaven. I can hardly wait for that day. Just as sap brings new life to a tree in the springtime, Jesus will bring new and eternal life to us when He comes the second time.

Pour It On

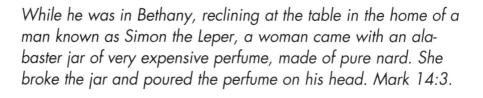

While he was in Bethany, reclining at the table in the home of a man known as Simon the Leper, a woman came with an alabaster jar of very expensive perfume, made of pure nard. She broke the jar and poured the perfume on his head. Mark 14:3.

Today's verse is almost exactly like the verse we read on October 4. Let me teach you something about the books of Matthew, Mark, Luke, and John on today's hike. You'll discover they sometimes told the same stories. Why would they do that? You see, even though Matthew and Mark both told the story of the woman who poured perfume on Jesus' head, there are differences in their stories. For instance, Matthew didn't tell us what kind of perfume the woman used—Mark did. He said it was nard, and today we'll learn a different lesson from the same story!

Nard is a sweet and spicy perfume made from plants that grow in the mountains of northern India. It's very hard to get to. This story took place in Israel. Not only did someone have to hike into the mountains of India and find the plant, but after they made the perfume they had to bring it all the way to Israel! No wonder it was so expensive!

Jesus traveled all the way from heaven for us. It was a very long and very hard trip. At the end of His trip, cruel men crucified Him. When you are tempted to complain because you have difficult things to do, remember the trip that Jesus made for you, and your life won't seem quite so hard.

Swimming Upstream

When he had finished speaking, he said to Simon, "Put out into deep water, and let down the nets for a catch." Luke 5:4.

I like to hike into the mountains, find a swirling river, and look for trout. Trout are beautiful fish, and there are many different kinds. One of my favorites is the rainbow trout. It has a rainbow of colors along its side. Trout aren't easy to find, though. You have to look for them in a special way.

In order to get close to trout, you must come up behind them. Trout face right into fast waters to catch their food. You must also stay low along the river's edge. If they see you while you're trying to sneak up on them, they swim quickly into deeper water. That's where the disciples found the fish in today's verse.

Life can be like swimming upstream. But sometimes our hardest times can bring the greatest blessings. Sometimes when life treats us badly, God puts something in our way that feeds us spiritually and makes us a better person. Jesus will never give us more than we can bear in His strength. He invites us to swim deep into His arms. He'll give us everything we need to swim straight into the tough currents of life.

15 OCTOBER

Make My Day

On another Sabbath he went into the synagogue and was teaching, and a man was there whose right hand was shriveled. . . . He looked around at them all, and then said to the man, "Stretch out your hand." He did so, and his hand was completely restored. Luke 6:6-10.

Step quietly with those hiking boots today. We're in the synagogue. A synagogue is a Jewish church. Look over there—it's Jesus. He's asking that man to stretch out his hand. Oh, look at that poor man's hand. It's all curled up. Jesus is saying something to the man and looking at all the teachers. Look at the man's hand! It's not curled up anymore. Jesus healed him, and the teachers are angry. They're upset because they think Jesus shouldn't have done that on the Sabbath. But Jesus is telling them that the Sabbath is a great time to do good things for other people.

What are your Sabbaths like? Why not see what you can do this Sabbath to help someone out? It might be your neighbor, or someone in the hospital, or a person without a home who lives in your city. The Sabbath is such a special day. Why not make this one even more special by helping someone out, as Jesus did?

only Sleeping

Meanwhile, all the people were wailing and mourning for her. "Stop wailing," Jesus said. "She is not dead but asleep." Luke 8:52.

Today we've hiked into a sad story. A little girl has died. When people die loved ones are very sad. Death happens because of sin. It takes place when the wonderful brain and the amazing heart that God made, stops. A person's body becomes still. They can't laugh or play or do their work any more. Yes, it's a very sad day when people die.

But look at today's verse again. This story is different. It's different because Jesus was there. Jesus surprised everyone by saying that the little girl wasn't really dead—she was only asleep. She was dead for the people who loved her because they couldn't wake her up. But, it's different for Jesus. He can start a heart that's been stopped and He can wake up a brain that hasn't been working. That's what He did for this little girl. He just "woke" her up and made everyone happy.

It will be like that when Jesus comes again for those who have loved Him. People whose hearts have stopped long ago will start to beat. People we love who have been resting in the ground will get up again. People will see fathers and mothers, grandpas and grandmas, brothers and sisters for the first time in many years. To me, it will be a miracle. For Jesus, they were just sleeping.

17 OCTOBER

You're One Smart Bird!

Consider the ravens: They do not sow or reap, they have no storeroom or barn; yet God feeds them. And how much more valuable you are than birds! Luke 12:24.

Have you ever heard anyone say, "He's one smart bird"? That means the person being talked about is very smart. Now, I don't know who made that saying up, and I don't know what smart bird they were talking about, but it could have been the raven. Ravens belong to the crow family. They look a lot like crows, but they're usually larger. They can be more than two feet long from head to toe!

And they are smart. If you were to hike by the sea, you'd find ravens that are so smart, they've learned to carry shellfish they've caught high into the air and drop them onto the rocks below. This cracks the shells open so they can eat what's inside. Amazing!

But as smart as the raven is, your brain is much smarter, and you are much more valuable to God. Just read today's verse again and see for yourself. Don't worry about a thing today. God is taking care of you and giving you all the smarts and power you need to make good decisions about your life. What a smart God we have!

A Shirt or a Robe?

He replied, "If you have faith as small as a mustard seed, you can say to this mulberry tree, 'Be uprooted and planted in the sea,' and it will obey you." Luke 17:6.

As we hike through the mulberry grove today, I want you to look carefully at the branches and leaves for little furry lumps. Those little lumps are cocoons—very special cocoons that expensive silk shirts are made from.

You see, silk moths lay their eggs only on mulberry leaves. When the eggs hatch, silkworms break out and start eating the leaves. The silkworms grow and grow until they're ready to turn into moths. Before they can turn into moths, though, they must spin a cocoon. That cocoon is the material that expensive silk ties, shirts, and robes are made from.

It might be nice to have a silk shirt, but a robe of righteousness is much better. God sent His Son, who lived a perfect life and died on the cross and rose again for us. That robe of righteousness cost far more than a silk shirt. But you and I only need to ask for it. It's absolutely free. Ask Jesus for that special robe today. He's already got one made for you.

Don't Sweat It

And being in anguish, he prayed more earnestly, and his sweat was like drops of blood falling to the ground. Luke 22:44.

There's one thing about all this hiking—it sure does make you sweat. No one I know really likes to sweat, but sweat is actually very important. Did you know sweat helps cool you down? When your skin is moist, and that moisture evaporates into the air, you feel cooler. Sweat also helps move poisons out of your body.

Today's verse tells a very sad story. Jesus' heart was hurting so much He was sweating. He was sweating so much it was like blood pouring down His skin from a cut. Jesus was hurting so much because He knew He was about to die on the cross. Of course that would hurt, but what hurt Him more was this: He didn't know if He would ever see His Father in heaven again. Sin sure does terrible things.

Today we can be so happy Jesus died for us. But we also need to realize how terrible sin is. It cost Jesus all that pain. His sweat was like blood. But He did it so you and I would never have to be separated from our Father in heaven like He was. So don't sweat it—Jesus died for you!

Ear Surgery

One of them struck the servant of the high priest, cutting off his right ear. But Jesus answered, "No more of this!" And he touched the man's ear and healed him. Luke 22:50, 51.

Just imagine hiking through the Garden of Gethsemane that night before Jesus died. You would have seen Peter pull out his sword and chop off a man's ear. Ouch. Then Jesus, the Great Physician, picked up the ear from the ground and put it back on the man's head. Amazing!

Did you know that reconstructive ear surgery is done today? Doctors have found ways to take skin and a bony material called cartilage from other parts of the body. Then they "build" ears for those who have lost them in an accident or who were born without them. God must have let them in on His secret for reconstructing ears. I'm glad He did.

Our God is so powerful. He made us so wonderfully, and He's let earth's doctors in on some of His "people-building instructions." God is an incredible Creator. See the "Doctor" today and let Him reconstruct your heart. He'll give you the same kind of heart that caused Jesus to love His enemies in the Garden of Gethsemane that night.

Just a Look

Just as Moses lifted up the snake in the desert, so the Son of Man must be lifted up. John 3:14.

Did you ever wonder why most people wear hiking boots in the wilderness? Actually, there are many reasons— protecting your feet from sharp rocks, keeping your feet dry, and preventing poisonous snakebites. But don't quit hiking because you think a snake might bite you. It actually doesn't happen very often.

The best thing to do if a poisonous snake bites you is to lie still while someone gets help or carries you to a hospital. Try not to move too much. When you arrive at the hospital, the doctors might give you antivenin. Antivenin is medicine that will help your body fight off the poisons in the snakebite.

The Israelites had gotten themselves in sin trouble again, and God allowed poisonous snakes to bite them. But God gave them a cure. He told Moses to make a snake out of brass and tell the people to look at it. All they had to do was look at it and they would be cured.

You and I have been bitten by sin. Jesus wants us to look to Him so He can cure us. Look to Jesus today and let Him give you the antivenin for sin.

I Never Get Tired . . .

Jacob's well was there, and Jesus, tired as he was from the journey, sat down by the well. It was about the sixth hour. John 4:6.

Whew, are you tired yet? We're almost to November, and we sure have hiked a long way this year. Have you ever been on a hike that made your muscles sore and tired? Do you know why your muscles get tired? Here are a couple of the reasons.

Your muscles—in fact, every part of your body—need air and water. When you hike a long way, your muscles sometimes need more water and air than you can give them, and they get tired. You also need fuel when you hike. Just as a car needs gas to run, your body needs the right foods to make it work properly. If you haven't been eating right, your muscles can't work like they're supposed to and can run out of fuel.

In today's verse we see that Jesus got tired just like we do. That means that as well as being God, He truly was a human being. He understands everything we go through. Aren't you glad He came to this earth as a real person to save us? I love to think about Jesus. That's one thing I'll never get tired of doing!

Bigger and Better

He cuts off every branch in me that bears no fruit, while every branch that does bear fruit he prunes so that it will be even more fruitful. John 15:2.

Today we're hiking through an orchard of fruit trees. It smells so sweet and delicious when the trees are blooming. Did you know that God is a gardener? He is! Just read today's verse. Now I can understand cutting off branches that don't grow any fruit, but did you know if a gardener cuts back the branches that do grow fruit, the tree will grow more and larger fruit? It's true. That's called pruning.

But Jesus wasn't really talking about fruit in this verse. He was using fruit as an example. He was really talking about people. He meant that sometimes we need to be pruned like a fruit tree. That means we need to learn lessons that are hard. When our parents or teachers have to punish us, it only makes us better boys and girls. Just as the fruit tree will grow better fruit after it's pruned, we'll be better people after we've learned some of the hard lessons of life.

So don't be afraid of hard things. Trust God to help you learn from those tough lessons. You'll be a better Christian who will grow more heavenly fruit for Him.

Forever Fresh

You did not choose me, but I chose you and appointed you to go and bear fruit—fruit that will last. Then the Father will give you whatever you ask in my name. John 15:16.

We ducked our heads as we passed through the creaky door and into the dark, sweet-smelling room. It took us underground. Our eyes adjusted to the darkness slowly, and soon we saw apples everywhere. Mr. Potter had taken us into his fruit cellar. He told us he could keep fruit fresh for a long time in that room. He picked up one apple and announced that it had been in the cellar for more than a year. It looked delicious. He said that because of the darkness and the cool temperature it would taste close to fresh even though it was more than a year old.

Today's verse talks about long-lasting fruit too. The fruit it's talking about is the new life and new heart that God gives us when we say yes to Him. This verse tells us something else wonderful. It shows us that Jesus chose us for His own. Doesn't that make you feel good all over? Jesus loves you and me so much. He chose us as His own, and He'll change us into loving people with lasting fruit—fruit that will last for eternity.

25 OCTOBER

Drink on a Stick

A jar of wine vinegar was there, so they soaked a sponge in it, put the sponge on a stalk of the hyssop plant, and lifted it to Jesus' lips. John 19:29.

They put a sponge soaked with vinegar on a hyssop branch and lifted it to Jesus' lips. Well, we know what vinegar is and we know what a sponge is, but what is hyssop?

Hyssop is a plant that people from long ago used for medicine. They would take the flowers from the plant, dry them, put them in boiling water, squeeze in a little honey, and drink hyssop tea. It is said to taste minty and help you feel better when you have a cold.

If we'd been hiking through Jerusalem on the day this verse is talking about, it would have been a very sad time for you and me. You see, it was the day Jesus died on the cross. They put that sponge soaked with vinegar on a hyssop branch to give Jesus something to drink. It doesn't sound like a very good drink to me. Jesus went through all that pain for you and me. He loves us so much. Thank Him today by choosing to live for Him. Your life will be much tastier than vinegar or hyssop tea.

Nets of Love

Simon Peter climbed aboard and dragged the net ashore. It was full of large fish, 153, but even with so many the net was not torn. John 21:11.

If you and I had been hiking along the shore on the day Peter caught all those big fish, we would have been shocked. Big fish have always amazed me. My friend Dan used to work on a fishing boat. Dan is a big guy. He's more than six feet tall. So when you look at my picture of him with a fish called a halibut that's bigger than he is, it's truly amazing.

Today's verse says that the net was full with 153 large fish and still not tearing. It must have been a very strong net. Jesus is like a strong net for us. When we're disappointed or angry or someone has wronged us, we can fall into the safety net of Jesus' arms. He'll keep life from tearing us apart.

The next time you see fishing boats, look for the nets. When you see them, remember that even though they will break with too many fish, Jesus will never give out on us or let us down. He's the strongest fisherman of all, and He's waiting to catch us in His nets of love.

27 OCTOBER

I Can't See

After he said this, he was taken up before their very eyes, and a cloud hid him from their sight. Acts 1:9.

I can remember hiking one time in the Adirondack Mountains of New York State. It was a cool, damp day. My friends, Dave and Debbie, and I were tired as we came close to the top of the mountain we were climbing. Finally we reached the top. We all gasped as we took in the view. Down below was a narrow valley between our mountain and the next mountain over. In the valley was a narrow strip of clouds. We were standing above the clouds!

Suddenly in the distance we heard a roar. Coming right at us were two Air Force fighter jets. All at once they darted down, turned upside down, and flew through the valley and the clouds, and off into the distance. It was the coolest thing!

For just a brief second, as the jets flew through the clouds, we couldn't see them. Even though clouds are made up of just water, they hid the jets from us. Sin can be like that too. It can look like fun, but it hides Jesus from our view. Don't let the clouds of sin hide Jesus from you. Keep yourself in clear skies and your eyes focused on Him.

Dreaming of You

*In the last days, God says, I will pour out my
Spirit on all people. Your sons and daughters
will prophesy, your young men will see visions,
your old men will dream dreams. Acts 2:17.*

Ah . . . After a long day of hiking, don't you just love to
lie down in your sleeping bag and drift off to sleep? I
sure do. There's nothing better when you're tired than to find a
comfortable place to rest your body and drift off to sleep. One
of the most unusual things we do when we sleep is dream. I've
had all kinds of dreams—good dreams, bad dreams, happy
dreams, and sad dreams.

In Bible times God used dreams to tell His people about the
future. He told Joseph a terrible famine was coming to Egypt.
He told Daniel what was going to happen to King
Nebuchadnezzar, and He told Peter that he should preach to
everyone, not just to the Jews.

It doesn't seem that God uses dreams that way quite as
much today, but we have His Word. It tells us about the future
too. It tells us that Jesus is coming soon. It tells us how to be
ready. Read His Word today and dream of the day He'll come
back to take you home.

The Promised Land

To this he replied: "Brothers and fathers, listen to me! The God of glory appeared to our father Abraham while he was still in Mesopotamia, before he lived in Haran." Acts 7:2.

Do you remember Abraham? He's the man in the Bible whom God asked to sacrifice his son Isaac. That must have been a very hard thing to do. I'm sure glad God didn't make Abraham go through with it.

God asked Abraham to do many difficult things. Our verse for today says that Abraham once lived in Mesopotamia. But God asked him to leave. That must have been very hard for Abraham to do. Mesopotamia was a beautiful land between two rivers. These rivers would overflow and bring very rich dirt for the people to grow their crops in. God asked him to leave this beautiful place and hike across a desert. But God blessed Abraham for obeying. He brought him to the Promised Land—a very rich land that God had promised to His people.

God wants to bless you, too. I don't know what He'll bless you with, but He will bless you. Things might not always be easy (like hiking across a desert), but one thing's for sure. If we trust in God, He will one day bring us to our Promised Land—a land called heaven.

Yum-yum

After taking some food, he regained his strength. Saul spent several days with the disciples in Damascus. Acts 9:19.

Today we're going to talk about hiking food. What kind of food would you take if you were on a long hike, like a backpacking trip—maybe dried noodles or dried fruit or powdered pudding? What? You don't think that sounds too good? What does sound good? What's your favorite food? Is it lasagna or corn on the cob or juicy strawberries? Whatever it is, it sure makes you feel better after you've eaten it. It gives you strength, doesn't it?

Today's verse tells us about Saul, who later became Paul. He was weak because he had met God. In fact, he was on the way to kill some of God's people. His meeting with God sort of took the strength right out of him. But after a few more meetings with God, some rest, and some good food, his strength returned.

Food is like that. It gives you the vitamins, minerals, and other things you need to keep your body running. Staying close to God is like that too. He gives you all the things you need to be a strong, healthy Christian. Make sure you eat your spiritual food from God's Word today and get strong in Him.

31 OCTOBER

Forgiveness Stronger Than a Hurricane

Before very long, a wind of hurricane force, called the "northeaster," swept down from the island. Acts 27:14.

Hang on to your hat; it'll be a windy hike today. I'll shout so you can hear my voice above the noise of the wind. If you'll read today's verse, you'll notice we're talking about a very strong storm. It's called a "northeaster." Some people call them nor'easters for short. Although the northeaster in our verse had winds of hurricane force, nor'easters and hurricanes are two different kinds of storms.

Hurricanes form in warm waters, and nor'easters form in cold waters. One thing's for sure: Both are very strong storms and can do a lot of damage. The nor'easter in today's verse was so powerful that it destroyed the ship Paul was sailing on. He was a prisoner under guard on that ship. Still he prayed for the people aboard and not one of them was lost.

Paul must have already forgiven the men who were holding him captive. Only God could help him do that. He didn't deserve to be in chains. All he was doing was telling others about the good news of Jesus.

Do you need to forgive someone today? Ask God to help you do it. He's got forgiveness stronger than a hurricane.

Waves of Miracles

The ship struck a sandbar and ran aground. The bow stuck fast and would not move, and the stern was broken to pieces by the pounding of the surf. Acts 27:41.

It's still windy today. We've hiked right up here on the shore because we're looking out to sea for Paul's ship. Look! It's over there—caught on that sandbar, and the waves are beating against it hard. Waves sure can be powerful! Oh, no! The back end of the boat just broke into thousands of pieces, and the people are grabbing whatever they can to float on. They're swimming to shore. Soon they'll be close enough so we can help them onto shore.

How terrible that must have been. The ship was breaking apart as the waves beat against it. And yet all of those on board were safe. No one drowned. No one died. Only God could perform a miracle like that. And guess what? God still performs miracles today.

For example, each day the miracle of new life takes place in hospitals. New life grows all around us. Best of all, God gives us new life each day to live for Him. Trust Jesus today, and He'll work waves of miracles in your life.

They're Waiting

The creation waits in eager expectation for the sons of God to be revealed. Romans 8:19.

Just think of what we've done this year. We've hiked through most of the Bible and looked at so much of God's creation. What a wonderful journey it's been! But look at today's verse. It says that creation is waiting for the sons of God to be revealed. It means that everything God has created has suffered because of sin and is waiting for the day that Jesus comes and re-creates everything new.

But why is it taking so long for Jesus to come again? The Bible says in 2 Peter 3:9, "He is patient with you, not wanting anyone to perish, but everyone to come to repentance." You see, God wants everyone in heaven with Him. Unfortunately, not everyone will choose to live forever in heaven. But God is being patient anyway, hoping that you and I and many more will choose to accept His love and grace.

Let's live each day for Jesus. Let's show Him how much we appreciate what He did for us when He died on the cross. Let's tell everyone we meet about Jesus so He and creation don't have to wait any longer.

He Thought of Everything

I am convinced that neither death nor life, neither angels nor demons, neither the present nor the future, nor any powers, neither height nor depth, nor anything else in all creation, will be able to separate us from the love of God that is in Christ Jesus our Lord. Romans 8:38, 39.

So far this year we've looked at all the things of nature we can see. Well, that makes sense, doesn't it? After all, how could we look at the things of nature we can't see? Let me tell you what I'm talking about. Can you think of anything God created that you can't normally see? There are probably many things, but today we're talking about angels.

God created angels to do special jobs. They take care of human beings, they deliver important messages for God, and sometimes they even help bring God's punishment. Angels are very mysterious.

Today's verse tells us that angels won't separate us from God's love. I know God's angels would never do that. They love us too much. I'm looking forward to the day when I meet the angels of heaven. God is so wonderful to have given us our special protectors. They help us every day to know more about God's love. God really thought of everything, didn't He?

The Fingerprint of God

Yet, . . . election might stand. Romans 9:11.

On our hike through today's verse we read about twins. The twins our verse is talking about were Jacob and Esau. You can read their story beginning with the second half of Genesis 25. Although they were twins, you'll see they were very different.

Do you know what twins are? They are two babies a mother carries in her body at the same time. Some twins are quite different; they are called fraternal twins. Some twins look almost alike; they are called identical twins. Identical twins have the same type of blood and hair. They're almost like each other in every way, but there are some differences. One may be more outgoing than the other, and their fingerprints are always different.

As Christians, you and I want to become like Jesus. We'll never be exactly like Jesus, just like twins are never exactly alike. But His love can still shine through our lives. People will see each day that we're becoming more like Him. Ask Jesus to make you more like Him today. Tell Him you'd like His fingerprint on you.

Two Trees in One

If some of the branches have been broken off, and you, though a wild olive shoot, have been grafted in among the others and now share in the nourishing sap from the olive root, do not boast. Romans 11:17, 18.

On today's hike we're going to see the most amazing thing. We're going to see two apple trees in one. You see, when Mr. Apple Grower grows an apple tree that produces very delicious apples, he wants to make sure his other trees do the same. So he cuts a branch from his best apple tree. He then makes a small hole in the trunk of a young apple tree and sticks that branch from his best tree into the hole. And guess what—it grows! It's called grafting.

God can put His life into yours, too. Oh, not quite like the apple grower does with an apple branch. I just know when God's life is placed into yours, you will become a better person. You'll be kinder. You'll be more loving. You'll be more giving. It won't be you. It will be God's power living in you. Ask Him today to graft His life into yours. Ask Him to help you grow into a Christian who will lead others to the great Person Grower—Jesus.

Heart Gardens

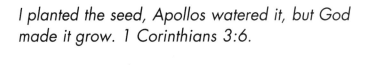

I planted the seed, Apollos watered it, but God made it grow. 1 Corinthians 3:6.

Careful now. Make sure as you're hiking through my garden, you don't step on the plants. Do you see the corn and the beans and the squash? We are going to have so many deliciously fresh vegetables for so many meals this summer. I can hardly wait for everything to be ready.

Today's verse talks about another kind of garden—the garden of the heart. Paul said when he preached from the Bible it was like planting the seed of life in someone's heart. Apollos, another church member, watered the people's hearts. That means he helped them understand what it was like to be a Christian and helped them along the way. The last part of our verse is the most important. God makes us grow as Christians. No one else can do it. Just as no one else but God can make vegetables grow, no one else but God can make His Word grow in our hearts and lives.

God really is the greatest gardener in the universe. Plant His Word in your heart, water it by learning more about Him, and watch God grow you into becoming more like Him each day.

Feeding the Shepherd

Who serves as a soldier at his own expense? Who plants a vineyard and does not eat of its grapes? Who tends a flock and does not drink of the milk? 1 Corinthians 9:7.

Today our hike takes us into the barn. It smells sort of funny in here, but that's just the way cows smell. Have you ever noticed those bags on the cow's tummies with those fingerlike things hanging down? That's where cow's milk comes from. The calves (or babies) use those "fingers" just like human babies use bottles. They're filled with delicious milk.

In today's verse Paul says a person who has cows or goats should get to drink their milk. Paul was actually telling the people that the pastor of their church should have enough to eat and drink too. Our pastors work hard to build our churches. We are the flock, and we need to give them something back. We need to pray for them; we need to give our tithes and offerings to help pay our pastors for their work; and we need to help our pastors spread the good news of Jesus.

Let your pastor know you care about them today. Take a minute right now and write them a letter telling them you're glad they're the shepherd of your flock.

Plowing for Souls

When the plowman plows and the thresher threshes, they ought to do so in the hope of sharing in the harvest. 1 Corinthians 9:10.

When I was a teenager I lived on a farm. All around us were miles and miles of fields where sugar beets, corn, and soybeans grew. Each spring I'd watch the farmers drive their big tractors back and forth across the fields digging their plows into the ground. Why did they do it? Why not just throw some seed out there and wait for it to grow?

Farmers know the soil must be prepared if the crops they are planting are to grow strong and healthy. The dirt needs to be loosened up so air and water can reach the roots of the plants. Fertilizer is also plowed into the ground so the crops will have plenty of plant food. Without plowing, there would be no harvest.

Just like the ground must be prepared for crops, people's hearts must be prepared to accept Jesus. Maybe you can be like a plowman and introduce people to Jesus. Maybe a pastor will baptize that person someday. Keep plowing for Jesus and watch God, the Great Farmer, grow beautiful crops to harvest for His kingdom.

Two Left Feet

*Now the body is not made up of one part but of many. . . .
But in fact God has arranged the parts in the body, every one
of them, just as he wanted them to be. If they were all one
part, where would the body be? 1 Corinthians 12:14-19.*

Have you ever stumbled and fallen as you've hiked? When you fell, did someone say to you, "Do you have two left feet?" Or did you ever hear someone say, "I'm all thumbs"? Now, those people didn't really mean you had two left feet or that they had only thumbs. They just meant that they were clumsy.

Today's verse says that God arranged the parts of our body just perfectly so they could each do their job. In our churches God has given us each a job to do, just like the parts of the body. Some people are very good at leading music, while some are very good at teaching Bible lessons. Still others are very good at making the church lawn beautiful. God made us each the way He wanted us. We can each help in our own way in God's church. Let's learn to respect one another for the talents God has blessed us with and encourage one another to play their part in the body of Christ.

Be a Star!

The sun has one kind of splendor, the moon another and the stars another; and star differs from star in splendor. 1 Corinthians 15:41.

The blacksmith's shop was often the center of town in the old western United States. People would hike for miles around to get their metal things made or fixed. Blacksmiths made horseshoes, fixed wagon wheels, and made metal rings to tie horses to the hitching post.

To make all these things the blacksmith had to get the metal very hot. As the blacksmith heated the metal it changed colors. It started out black, then it turned orange, and finally it was so hot it turned white.

If you'll look at today's verse, you'll see that stars do the same thing. Different stars are hotter than others. When you see them through a telescope some look white, some blue, others orange, and some yellow. They're all different temperatures.

As we get more excited about Jesus, people will see changes in our "temperature" too. The hotter we are and the more excited we get about Jesus, the more we want to tell others about Him. If we aren't very excited about Jesus, people may not even realize that we're His followers. Be a star on fire for Jesus today and tell everyone you know how bright His love for them is.

There's Nothin' Sweeter

Thanks be to God, who always leads us in triumphal procession in Christ and through us spreads everywhere the fragrance of the knowledge of him. For we are to God the aroma of Christ among those who are being saved and those who are perishing. 2 Corinthians 2:14, 15.

Have you ever hiked through a field and picked flowers for your mother? Did you put them in a vase and fill it with water? Did the flowers create a sweet smell in your house? Have you ever noticed that different flowers have different smells, or aromas? The aroma of a flower is its smell. I love the aroma of roses. They have a sweet smell that can fill a whole room.

Knowing about Jesus gives life a sweet aroma, too. Everything seems better when you know Him. Even if things aren't going so well, Jesus makes life sweeter.

The sad thing is, there are many people who don't know how sweet life can be with Jesus. If you'll look at today's verse, it tells us there are some who are perishing. That means they won't go to heaven unless they find out about Jesus. It's up to us to tell them. Tell someone today so they'll find out there's nothing sweeter than Jesus.

12 NOVEMBER

From Slime to Shine!

We have this treasure in jars of clay to show that this all-surpassing power is from God and not from us. 2 Corinthians 4:7.

Ooh, yuck! What a sticky, slimy mess. We're hiking in clay today. If you've ever stepped in wet clay, you know what I'm talking about. Clay is actually made up of tiny particles of rock that are so small the wind can blow them for miles. When those tiny particles get wet, they become slippery and slimy.

Now, you might be wondering what good a sticky, slimy mess like that could be, but clay is actually very useful. When clay is wet, it can be formed into many different shapes. After an object is formed, it is allowed to dry and then put into a very hot oven. This bakes the object and makes it very hard. You probably have clay pots or statues somewhere in your house. This is how they were made.

Our verse tells us there can be treasure in jars of clay. It's not talking about the same kind of clay we've been hiking in, though. It's talking about us. We are like clay pots. Sort of plain and dirty with sin, but with Jesus in our lives we are a treasure. In fact, you could say that with Jesus we've gone from slime to shine!

Wear Your Robe

I have labored and toiled and have often gone without sleep; I have known hunger and thirst and have often gone without food; I have been cold and naked. 2 Corinthians 11:27.

Poor Paul. As we hike though today's verse we discover he had some pretty hard times. He had been hungry, sleepy, cold, and naked because he chose to be faithful to Jesus.

Have you ever been really cold before? I heard a story about a man who was driving through a winter storm. The snow fell so heavily that he couldn't see to drive anymore. He pulled his car to the side of the road. The snow kept falling and eventually covered his car. He kept the car running to keep warm, but it soon ran out of gas. The man made a mistake by not wearing a very warm coat and not bringing any food with him. He soon was shivering, and the temperature of his body dropped. This is called hypothermia. He soon became very still and almost died when, just in time, a man driving a snowplow discovered him.

Satan wants us to get Christian hypothermia. He wants our love for Jesus to fall asleep and die. Don't let that happen. Keep moving, put on Jesus' warm robe of righteousness, and stay on fire for Him.

Get Some Fruit of Your Own

The fruit of the Spirit is love, joy, peace, patience, kindness, goodness, faithfulness, gentleness and self-control. Galatians 5:22, 23.

If you'll look back on our hikes through this book, you'll find we've talked about fruit quite often. That's because God talks about fruit so much. Today He wants us to eat some more fruit, and let me tell you—it is delicious! Today we're going to talk about the fruit of the Spirit. And it's true: Your life will be so much more delicious if you have this fruit.

In Galatians 5:22, 23 God compares the blessings of the Holy Spirit with fruit. I think He does that because He knows if you have love for others, if joy is filling your heart, and if you help bring peace to those who are fighting, you will be a delicious person to the people around you. Only Jesus can make you this kind of deliciously fruity person. Only He can give you the fruit of the Holy Spirit.

Jesus makes life so wonderful! There are so many people who aren't happy because they don't have the Spirit's fruit. Let Jesus grow some Spirit fruit on you today. Once others see what you've got, they won't be able to resist getting some fruit of their own.

Watch His Love Grow

Do not be deceived: God cannot be mocked.
A man reaps what he sows. Galatians 6:7.

Today we're back hiking in the garden. I just love gardens. There are so many different plants and vegetables and flowers. When I plant my garden I always put little wooden sticks with the name of the plants written on them. It helps me remember what I've planted. And guess what? The right plants always come up in the right places. I've never had bean plants come up where I've planted squash plants, and I've never had corn plants come up where I've planted tomato plants. Like today's verse says, "A man reaps what he sows." That means whatever you plant is exactly what grows.

For Christians it means when you plant Jesus in your heart, His love will grow there. If you plant sin in your heart, evil will grow. You must make the choice. Jesus wants you to choose Him. He knows if His love is growing in you, your life will be so much happier. Remember, your life will grow into whatever you plant in your heart. Plant Jesus today and watch His love grow in you.

16 NOVEMBER

What a Workout!

I pray also that the eyes of your heart may be enlightened in order that you may know . . . his incomparably great power for us who believe. That power is like the working of his mighty strength. Ephesians 1:18, 19.

Today we're back hiking where the strong people are. We're hiking into a gym where men and women lift weights. Do you see their muscles bulge? Do you see the people climbing the stair machines? They're all working very hard, aren't they? They want their hearts and bodies to get stronger.

Today's verse talks about the strongest person in the whole universe. It's Jesus, of course. Jesus has great power for everyone who believes in Him. He has power to help us overcome sin; He has power to defeat Satan; and He has the power to take us to heaven to live with Him forever. Jesus really has mighty strength.

It's important that you and I get plenty of exercise to make our bodies strong. We should also get plenty of brain exercise to make us smart people. Most important, we need to get Jesus in our life so we will have His mighty strength to defeat Satan and fly all the way to heaven with Him. Now, that will be quite a workout!

Who Let the Dogs Out?

Watch out for those dogs, those men who do evil, those mutilators of the flesh. Philippians 3:2.

In our house we have a puppy. We love him so much. He's a white furry ball named Ricci. He snuggles up next to us on the couch, turns over on his back, and begs us to rub his tummy. He sleeps on our beds during the day and tries to eat our food at the supper table. He must think he's a person. What a dog!

There are other types of dogs that aren't as friendly as Ricci, though. One of them is the dingo. The dingo is a wild dog that lives in Australia. Dingoes eat kangaroos, wallabies, and rabbits. They are ferocious killers. Some people in Australia once built a fence 3,000 miles long to keep the dingoes out. If you ever hike in Australia, stay away from the dingoes.

In today's verse Paul tells us to watch out for people who are like wild dogs. They tear people apart and do evil. Paul tells us to watch out for them because he knows they are Satan's helpers and want to destroy God's people. Stick close to Jesus. He'll keep the wild dogs away from you.

Tears of Love!

As I have often told you before and now say again even with tears, many live as enemies of the cross of Christ. Philippians 3:18.

Sometimes it's just downright sad. We've hiked through the Bible this year and learned so many wonderful things about God. So what's sad about that? What's sad is that so many people still live their lives as enemies of Jesus. Just look at today's verse. Paul was crying big tears for those people.

Sometimes the things God's enemies do can make us angry. That's a very natural thing to feel. But as we draw closer to Jesus, He will turn our anger into tears. God gave us tears to help us feel sadness. And it's hard to be angry with someone when you feel sadness for them.

You see, Jesus changes everything about us. He changes bad things into good; He changes anger into forgiveness; He changes hate into love. How do I know that? Because Paul, the one who wrote today's verse, actually killed Christians. He hated them. He wanted to get rid of them all. But Jesus changed his life completely.

God's love is a very amazing thing. It's the most powerful thing in the entire world. Let Jesus come into your heart and change your anger to tears of love.

The Foot Bone's Con-nected to the Leg Bone

He has lost connection with the Head, from whom the whole body, supported and held together by its ligaments and sinews, grows as God causes it to grow. Colossians 2:19.

Have you ever heard the song that goes, "The foot bone's connected to the leg bone; the leg bone's connected to the hip bone," and on and on? Did you ever wonder how your bones were connected to each other? Well, take a look at our verse for the day—the answer is right there. Did you guess ligaments? If you did, you're right!

Ligaments are tough but flexible bands that connect your bones together. They have to be tough, or your bones would pull apart from each other. They also have to be flexible, or you'd walk a little funny. Think of how hard it would be to move if your bones were glued together solidly.

As important as ligaments are, your head is the most important part of your body. That's where your brain is, and your brain controls everything. We as Christians are part of Christ's body, or the church. We must stay connected to the Head of the church. The Head of the church is Jesus. Stay connected to Him, because He's the one who holds us all together.

Tasty Words

Let your conversation be always full of grace, seasoned with salt, so that you may know how to answer everyone. Colossians 4:6.

Well, we've hiked once again into the salt mines. We've talked about salt once earlier this year, and we'll talk about it one more time before this year is over. Salt was used for many different things in Bible times. It was used to preserve food, scrape meat from animal hides, and as today's verse tells us, it was used to season food—to make food taste better.

When people put it on their food, it has to be just the right amount. Too much salt makes food taste terrible. Too little, and food may taste too plain. Just the right amount helps food taste so much better for many people.

Today's verse talks about putting salt on our words. What that really means is when you speak to others with kindness and love and respect, they'll listen to you. They'll listen because they know you care for them. That's so important. When God gives you a chance to tell others about Jesus, you'll want them to be listening. Put some salt on your words today. Speak kindly to others. Then tell them about Jesus.

Toasty Warm

Do not put out the Spirit's fire. 1 Thessalonians 5:19.

We're talking about fire again today as we hike through the wilderness. Fire was very important to the people of the Bible. In fact, it was so important that we'll talk about it again tomorrow. We've found out the Israelites used fire for melting and forming metal objects, cooking, heat, and light.

When an Israelite camper built a fire it started out small. First, small shavings of wood were set on fire. Then bigger and bigger branches were placed in the fire. Finally larger logs were thrown in, so the fire would burn for a long time.

God's Holy Spirit is trying to build a fire in you. He starts out small by helping you understand simple things about God like His love for you. As you grow older and get to know God better, the Holy Spirit teaches you more and more until your fire for God is burning brightly and will last a long time.

Our verse today tells us not to put out the Spirit's fire. Don't put out your fire for Jesus by choosing sin instead of the Spirit. Don't let Satan fool you into believing that his ways are better than God's. Let the Spirit's fire keep you toasty warm until Jesus comes again.

22 NOVEMBER

What a Relief It Is

Give relief to you who are troubled, and to us as well. This will happen when the Lord Jesus is revealed from heaven in blazing fire with his powerful angels. 2 Thessalonians 1:7.

On yesterday's hike we talked about building a fire and starting out small. If you kept adding bigger and bigger logs to the fire, you'd soon have a giant blaze, wouldn't you? Think of how good that would feel on a cold night after hiking for miles. It would warm you up inside and out.

Today's verse talks about another blazing fire—the blazing fire of Jesus' second coming. What a sight that will be! Some people will be frightened, but for those of us who know Jesus our verse says it will be a relief. No more sin, no more sadness, no more crying—it will be even better than the relief of a blazing fire at the end of a cold hike.

Jesus wants us to look forward with excitement to His soon coming. He doesn't want us to be afraid. He loves us and wants to take us to heaven with Him. He's on our side. Put yourself on His side today and get ready for the relief of the warmest fire of all—the second coming of Jesus.

Thank You

The Scripture says, "Do not muzzle the ox while it is treading out the grain," and "The worker deserves his wages." 1 Timothy 5:18.

Have you ever seen an ox? An ox is a name used for several members of the cow family. In Bible times they were used to pull wagons and plows and do other work. One of the jobs farmers had their oxen do was grind grain. An ox would turn a heavy stone round and round. This heavy stone sat on top of another heavy stone with grain in between. As the ox turned the stone the grain was ground into flour. The flour was used to bake bread.

Our verse for the day says the ox should not be muzzled. That means its mouth should not be closed tight and kept from eating. The Bible says that since the ox is working hard it should be able to eat.

Paul was also trying to say to Timothy that pastors work hard and should be appreciated for their hard work. Why don't you let your pastor know how much you appreciate their hard work? Thank them for leading you and your family closer to Jesus. Why not call them today and thank them?

Money, Money, Money

The love of money is a root of all kinds of evil. Some people, eager for money, have wandered from the faith and pierced themselves with many griefs. 1 Timothy 6:10.

Last month we talked about roots on one of our hikes. We said if our roots weren't put deep into Jesus, we would be dying Christians. On today's hike we're going to talk about one of the other places people grow their roots. If you've read today's verse, you know it's money.

Putting your roots into money means that most everything you do is to get money. Some people just love money. They love spending it; they love saving it; they love complaining about it; they love everything about money.

Today's verse says that loving money can get you into trouble. Some who have put their roots in money have even wandered away from God. Their life has turned to sadness because they made money their god.

It's very important to notice this verse doesn't say that money is bad; it says that *loving* money is bad. God has given us money as a blessing to help our families and others. Just remember this—love God and love people and use your money to help both.

Breathe Deeply and Live

All Scripture is God-breathed and is useful for teaching, rebuking, correcting and training in righteousness. 2 Timothy 3:16.

One thing that is very important while we're on this year-long hike is breathing. It would be pretty hard to hike if you weren't breathing, wouldn't it? It's important to breathe in deeply. That's call inhaling. Then it's important to breathe out. That's called exhaling. It's important to breathe out so you'll have room for new, fresh air in your lungs. It's also important because the plants you see all around you use the air you breathe out. It's called carbon dioxide, and it brings life to all the plants in our world.

Today's verse tells us about something God breathed out that gives us life too—eternal life. It's the Bible. Our verse says that God breathed out the words of the Bible. It also says they are good for teaching lessons, helping us to see when we sin, and helping us to be better people. All that came from God's breath.

Just as plants live from what we breathe out, we live from what God breathed out. The Holy Bible leads us to God, and He gives us eternal life—the best life of all. So breathe deeply from God's Word today and live.

26 NOVEMBER

Which Is It?

The reason I left you in Crete was that you might straighten out what was left unfinished and appoint elders in every town, as I directed you. Titus 1:5.

Today we're going to hike on the island of Crete. Crete is a large island in the Mediterranean Sea. Today's verse tells us that Paul left Titus on Crete with a job to do. I'm sure that while Titus was on the island of Crete he took some quiet time nature hiking with God.

One of the plants Titus may have seen on his hikes is the carob plant. The carob plant grows little carob beans that taste a lot like chocolate. You may have had a carob brownie or a carob bar or maybe even carob cake. Carob tastes almost like chocolate, but it doesn't have some of the things that aren't so good for you that chocolate has.

There are many things in life that look very much alike. Often one is better for us than the other. We need to check with Jesus every day to help us make good decisions for our life. He knows what's best, and He'll show us which decision we should make. So the next time you need to make a tough decision, ask God to show you the difference between the chocolate and the carob.

Older and Wiser

I appeal to you on the basis of love. I then, as Paul—an old man and now also a prisoner of Christ Jesus—I appeal to you. Philemon 1:9, 10.

Today we're hiking in the little book of Philemon. In it we discover that Paul is an old man. Some say his eyesight was going bad. He may not have been able to move as quickly as when he was young, and he probably had aches and pains most of the time. But even though Paul couldn't do some of the things he could when he was younger, he had some things you only get when you're old.

Paul had known God for many years now and just like any good friend, the longer you know them, the more you love them. Because Paul and God had known one another for so many years, they loved each other very much.

There are some parts of getting old that aren't much fun, but you and I can learn from those who have grown older in Jesus. Ask them how to be a better Christian. Ask them what they've learned from God. Let them know you respect them because they have been faithful to Jesus. Then look forward, with them, to when Jesus comes again to take young and old to heaven with Him.

Learn Something New Every Day

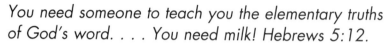

You need someone to teach you the elementary truths of God's word. . . . You need milk! Hebrews 5:12.

When you were just a baby hiker, do you know what you ate for breakfast, lunch, and supper? You probably drank some kind of milk or formula. It was soft and smooth. You didn't eat pizza or crackers or even vegetables. You had no teeth, and your body wasn't ready to digest that hard food yet. After a while you began eating vegetables. But someone had to mash them up until they were smooth and soft. Finally, as you grew older you began to eat harder foods, such as toast and crackers.

Being a child of God is much the same. Today's verse says we must first learn the simple things of God. All the things we've been learning on our hike through the Bible this year are the simple things of God. But there's so much more. As you begin to grow older and wiser, you will understand even more about God. In fact, if you keep hiking through God's Word, you'll never stop learning more about Him no matter how old you get.

Don't worry if you don't understand everything yet. Keep studying about God and His love for you and learn something new every day.

Dusty Hearts

Land that drinks in the rain often falling on it and that produces a crop useful to those for whom it is farmed receives the blessing of God. Hebrews 6:7.

If you and I were to hike near my home during the dry part of the summer, we would see lots of dust blowing in the wind. Much of Colorado is often called the high desert because we get so little rain. The drier the ground gets, the harder it gets. Sometimes when it does rain, the water just runs off the top of the hardened ground and into the rivers. It never soaks into the earth very far. It takes many days of rain to soften the earth enough for the rain to soak in.

When people get too busy for God and stay away from Him for a long time, their hearts can become like hardened ground. When God tries to speak, some people don't hear. God's words aren't soaking into their heart very far, because they've become hardened to Him.

I'm happy to say that God doesn't give up on us, though. Even if our hearts have become hard, He keeps pouring on His love until it breaks through and soaks in. Let Jesus soften your heart today. If you do that, you'll never have a dusty heart.

30 NOVEMBER

Parting With Problems

By faith the people passed through the Red Sea as on dry land. Hebrews 11:29.

Today we're hiking through the desert with the children of Israel. Finally the Egyptians have let us go free. Wow! Look at that huge sea up ahead of us. It's the Red Sea. How are we going to get across? Wait, what do I hear? Look at the clouds of dust rising into the sky. Oh no, it's the Egyptians coming after us with swords and spears. Wait. Listen to what Moses is saying. He's telling us to be still and watch God fight for us. How can God save us? There are mountains and desert and sea and Egyptians all around us. Where will we go?

Look, a dark cloud is coming down from heaven. I can't see the Egyptians anymore. What's Moses doing now? He's raising his shepherd's staff over the Red Sea. I don't believe it! I can see the sand on the bottom of the Red Sea. The water is standing up. This is amazing. We're walking across the bottom of the Red Sea on dry land. Isn't God good?

Sometimes problems come our way and it seems there's no way out. But God always has a way. Trust in Him today and watch Him part your problems.

Power to Decide

Strengthen your feeble arms and weak knees. Hebrews 12:12.

You know, we've been hiking almost one year together now. There's only a month to go. You and I have done exactly what this verse says we should do. We've hiked a long way and strengthened our arms and knees. We've also strengthened our legs and our hearts and our minds. We can be so thankful that Jesus has all the spiritual strength we need.

But why have we done all this exercise? Why have we spent all this time learning more about God and exercising our bodies and minds? It's because we need strength to make good decisions. You will have many decisions to make in your life. Each day you'll need to make a decision to let Jesus into your heart. There will also be times people ask you to do things you shouldn't. You'll have to make a decision to say no. In order to make the right decisions you will need to be strong. That's why we've done all this spiritual exercise.

When you make the decision to do the right thing, something wonderful happens. Jesus gives you power to do the right thing. So stick with Jesus. He's got all the muscles you need to make the right decisions on your earthly hike.

What a Trick!

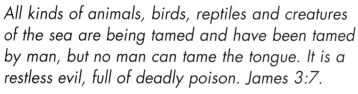

All kinds of animals, birds, reptiles and creatures of the sea are being tamed and have been tamed by man, but no man can tame the tongue. It is a restless evil, full of deadly poison. James 3:7.

On at least one of our hikes together, I told you about my dog, Ricci. My children, Kristen, Chris, and Michael, have managed to teach Ricci a couple of tricks. If they hold a treat above his head and tell him to sit, he sits. If they tell him to speak, he speaks. Some dogs can roll over and catch Frisbees. Ricci hasn't learned how to do that yet.

But even though we can teach animals some pretty amazing things, our verse says that no man can tame the tongue. Have you ever said something you know you shouldn't have said? We try so hard to say the right things, but sometimes we really make a mess with our words.

Only Jesus can give us the power to say the right things. Our hearts are sinful, and that's why we say things we shouldn't. Jesus can change our hearts and cause us to say the right things. Ask Jesus to tame your tongue today. For Him, that's a trick that's no trouble at all.

Springing Words

*Out of the same mouth come praise and cursing.
My brothers, this should not be. Can both fresh water
and salt water flow from the same spring? James 3:10, 11.*

Way back in January we talked about springs. Most springs have clear, fresh water coming from them, but there are some saltwater springs. There's a saltwater spring in the United States in Ohio. This spring is salty, because before the water comes to the surface it passes through rock salt buried underground.

Today's verse tells us that just like you'll find one type of water, fresh or salt, coming from a spring in the earth, we should find only one type of words springing from our mouths. We shouldn't find evil words and good words coming out of the same mouth. Unfortunately, that happens with all of us at times, doesn't it?

Each day we need to grow closer and closer to Jesus. We need to ask Him to help us with the words that come from our mouth. We need to read His Word so it's stuck in our head. Just like saltwater springs from salt in the earth, words of praise spring from a mind filled with God. Fill your brain with Jesus today, and words of praise will come springing out.

Jesus Won't Corrode

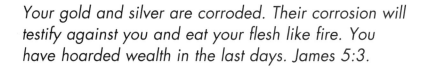

Your gold and silver are corroded. Their corrosion will testify against you and eat your flesh like fire. You have hoarded wealth in the last days. James 5:3.

As we finish our hike through the book of James we read some hard words. James is talking to someone who has gold and silver. He's telling them their gold will corrode. Do you know what corrosion is? Have you ever seen rusty metal? Rust is corrosion. It happens when metal and damp air touch each other. The air actually eats the metal. But air is everywhere, isn't it? So why isn't all metal rusting? It's because most metal is covered with paint or another material that keeps the air from touching it.

Some people are very worried about having lots of money. The Bible tells us that God will take care of us and that we shouldn't worry about having enough money. Today's verse tells us that gold and silver will corrode anyway. When we die our money won't do us any good. It won't buy us anything in heaven. Jesus is all that matters. He won't get old. He won't corrode. He won't let us down. As you and I wait for Jesus to come again, let's not worry about such things as money. Jesus will give us everything we need.

Which Is Worth More?

You know that it was not with perishable things such as silver or gold that you were redeemed from the empty way of life handed down to you from your forefathers, but with the precious blood of Christ, a lamb without blemish or defect. 1 Peter 1:18, 19.

We hike into a new book today—the book of 1 Peter. It looks like Peter and James have the same thing on their minds. Yesterday James told us that having lots of gold and silver won't matter when Jesus comes again. Today Peter is telling us that gold and silver will perish. That means they will be destroyed. How will they be destroyed? They'll be destroyed along with the rest of the earth when Jesus comes again. That may sound like a bad thing, but actually it's a good thing. It's a good thing because Jesus is going to make everything new for us.

If you'll read today's verse, you'll see Peter is trying to tell us that gold and silver aren't even as valuable as blood. The blood Peter is talking about is the blood of Jesus. When Jesus died for us on the cross, His blood became the most valuable thing on earth. It's valuable because it bought our ticket to heaven, and that's something gold or silver could never do.

Help, I'm Lost!

You were like sheep going astray, but now you have returned to the Shepherd and Overseer of your souls. 1 Peter 2:25.

Today we're hiking through a pasture to learn lessons from sheep. While sheep provide humans with wool for clothing, meat for food, and milk for cheese, I have to tell you something about them. Now, don't tell any sheep I told you this, but in some ways sheep aren't very smart. They're very easily frightened. If a piece of paper blows through the air by them, they'll run. If they get caught in a stream, they won't have any idea what they should do and may drown in very little water. And sadly, if the building they're in catches fire, they might just stand there and die. There's no doubt: sheep need our complete protection.

Don't get to feeling too good about yourself, though. Today's verse tells us we're much like sheep. Peter tells us we are often like sheep wandering away from their shepherd. We follow our own ideas much too easily. But there is hope. Our Good Shepherd, Jesus, is standing right next to us just waiting for us to say "we love You, and we want You to save us." Talk to the Good Shepherd today. Tell Him you don't want to be lost anymore.

I Can See Forgiveness

He is nearsighted and blind, and has forgotten that he has been cleansed from his past sins. 2 Peter 1:9.

A few months ago I hiked to the eye doctor's office. The doctor told me I needed some reading glasses. I'm now joining many other people who wear glasses to see well.

Some people who wear glasses are nearsighted. To be nearsighted means you can only see things well that are close. It means you have trouble focusing your eyes on things that are far away.

Today's verse tells us that a person who has forgotten that his sins have been forgiven is nearsighted and blind. I think that means he can only focus on the thing that is closest to him—himself. You see, when we only think of our sins and ourselves, we just sin more. The Bible tells us we should focus on Jesus. It means we need to look away from ourselves and look to the only One who can save us from our sins.

If you've asked Jesus to forgive your sins, then they're forgiven. Isn't that a great feeling? If you haven't asked Jesus to forgive you, stop and ask Him right now and then believe they're gone. You can, because they are—Jesus promised it! Now you can see again.

8 DECEMBER

Don't You Forget!

I will always remind you of these things, even though you know them and are firmly established in the truth you now have. I think it is right to refresh your memory as long as I live in the tent of this body. 2 Peter 1:12, 13.

Do you remember what you ate for your last meal? Did you forget? Ah, now you remember. You used your memory to remember what you ate. Do you know what memory is? It's the part of your brain that helps you remember telephone numbers, words, and people's faces.

Think about what it would be like if you didn't have a memory. You couldn't remember where you live—you'd be lost all the time. You couldn't remember anything your mother or father or teacher told you. That's never happened to you, has it? You wouldn't even remember your name. That would be terrible!

In today's verse Peter was trying to get people to use their memories. He wanted them to remember that Jesus had forgiven them and saved them. He wanted to remind them that Jesus wanted them to tell others about Him. Peter was getting them to use their memories to remember the very best thing of all—that Jesus loved them. He loves you, too—and don't you forget it!

A Holy Example

We ourselves heard this voice that came from heaven when we were with him on the sacred mountain. 2 Peter 1:18.

We've hiked up mountains this year, but none quite like this one. The mountain Peter is talking about in this verse is called the Mount of Transfiguration. Peter was there and he was scared silly. You see, Jesus took Peter, James, and John on a hike up this high mountain. While they were up there they saw Moses and Elijah; they saw Jesus glow with heavenly light; and they heard God speak from heaven. I think I'd have been afraid too.

We've talked often on our hikes this year about our friendship with Jesus. He truly is our best friend. But we must also remember He is an awesome God. Just by walking up a mountain, He can make it holy. He can make our lives holy too. He wants us to be an example for everyone to see what God can do with a young boy or girl.

The only way you and I can become that kind of example is to be with Jesus, just like Peter, James, and John were with Him on that sacred mountain. Jesus makes everything He touches holy. Ask Him to make your life a holy example too.

Mr. Fred

*He was rebuked for his wrongdoing by a donkey—
a beast without speech—who spoke with a man's
voice and restrained the prophet's madness. 2 Peter 2:16.*

Years ago there was a television program about a talking horse. His name was Mr. Ed. Mr. Ed was very smart. In fact, he was often smarter than his owner. Whenever there was a problem to be solved, Mr. Ed's owner would go out to the barn and talk to him. Mr. Ed always seemed to have the right answer. That's TV!

I don't know where the creators of this television show got the idea for a talking horse, but maybe it was the Bible. Today's verse tells us about a talking donkey. Let's call him Mr. Fred.

We all know that donkeys can't talk, but the donkey in today's verse did. Or did he? Actually, I think God moved his lips and talked for him. Amazing, isn't it? God can even use a donkey to preach.

Now, I know if God can use a donkey to speak His words, He can certainly use you and me. All we need to do is say yes and allow God to speak through us. Someone needs to hear God's words today. Will you be like Mr. Fred and let God speak through you?

This then is how we know that we belong to the truth, and how we set our hearts at rest in his presence. 1 John 3:19.

Have you ever noticed when you're hiking that your heart beats faster? Your muscles need lots of oxygen when you hike. When your muscles need more of it, your heart pumps faster to get the oxygen-carrying blood to all the muscles in your body. Do you think it's a bad thing to make your heart work hard? It isn't. In fact, you should work your heart and make it pump faster each day for a little while. Why? Because you need to make it stronger. It must stay strong to be healthy.

Even though you need to work your heart some each day, you also need to rest it. If it worked too hard, too much, it would wear out sooner than it should. It's important to rest it, too.

Today's verse talks about resting our hearts in Jesus. It means if we belong to Him, we don't need to worry if He can save us. We know He can! It's important to work hard in sharing Jesus with those around us, but we can rest our hearts knowing He will save us.

Hiking for Love

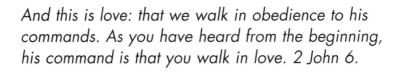

And this is love: that we walk in obedience to his commands. As you have heard from the beginning, his command is that you walk in love. 2 John 6.

On today's hike we're going to talk about how good hiking is for you. Many doctors say that hiking and walking are the very best exercises for you. They work your heart; they work your legs; and if you swing your arms while you walk or hike, they even work the muscles of your upper body. Another reason walking and hiking are such good exercises is that they don't shock your body the way running does. When you run, the joints in your knees and hips and feet are shocked each time your feet hit the ground.

Today's verse talks about walking in love. John tells us that walking in love means to obey God's commands. One of God's commands is that we love one another. When we love one another we won't be rude and shocking. We will be kind and gentle. We may have to firmly say no to someone who wants us to disobey God, but we will always do it kindly and lovingly. Hike some today to keep your heart healthy, and walk in love to bless the hearts of others.

Healthy in God

*Dear friend, I pray that you may enjoy good
health and that all may go well with you,
even as your soul is getting along well. 3 John 2.*

As we hike through the book of 3 John, we discover that
John was a very thoughtful person. Along with teaching
people the things of God, he also prayed that everything would
go well with them and that they would be in good health. What
a nice guy!

Do you know what it means to be in good health? It's no
fun to be sick, is it? Don't you feel so much better when you're
strong and healthy? Can't you do so much more and think so
much better when your stomach and your head and all the rest
of your body is feeling well?

Good health is no accident. You need to eat the right foods,
drink plenty of water, get lots of exercise, and get a good
night's sleep each night. Those are the "laws of good health."

Just like there are laws of good health, there are laws for
staying healthy in God. To be healthy in God, we need to talk
to Him often, read what He's written in His Word, and tell others about Him. Do it today. You'll feel so much better.

Watch the Blessings Grow

These men are blemishes at your love feasts, eating with you without the slightest qualm—shepherds who feed only themselves. They are clouds without rain, blown along by the wind; autumn trees, without fruit and uprooted—twice dead. Jude 12.

Today we begin our hike in the very short book of Jude—the next-to-the-last book of the Bible. Jude tells us a very sad story in today's verse. He talks about members of the church who were "clouds without rain."

When farmers plant their crops, they hope clouds full of rain will blow over their fields and water their plants. They aren't very happy when "clouds without rain" blow over.

But what did Jude mean when he said there were people who were like clouds without rain? He meant there are some people who do everything for themselves. They don't look to bless or help others in any way. It's a sad, sad thing to have that happen in our churches, isn't it?

God wants us to be clouds with lots of rain to bless others. Don't worry about others who may be looking out only for themselves; look for those you can bless with a smile, a helping hand, and a loving word. Be a cloud full of rain and watch the blessings grow.

Clean Up the Foam

*They are wild waves of the sea,
foaming up their shame. Jude 13.*

I love to hike along the ocean. I love the sound of the waves crashing on the shore. I love to look into the water and find shells and fish and driftwood. The ocean is a wonderful place God has created for us to enjoy.

If you've been to the ocean, you might have noticed foam along the shore. Many times this foam is caused by pollution in the ocean. Pollution is the garbage and chemicals that people throw into the water. What a sad thing to do. Why would someone want to throw garbage into God's beautiful creation? Sadly, people do it every day.

Sometimes people throw garbage into their minds. They read books and magazines and watch television programs that talk about things God wants us to stay away from. Today's verse says these people are like "waves of the sea, foaming up their shame." Just like the sea foams up with the garbage people throw into it, we will foam up with shame if we throw garbage into our minds. Choose to put only the things of God into your mind. Keep your thoughts crystal clear, just the way God made the ocean.

Hurts to Happiness

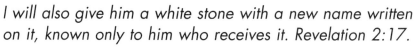

I will also give him a white stone with a new name written on it, known only to him who receives it. Revelation 2:17.

Our verse today sounds mysterious, doesn't it? Did you read the part that talks about a white stone with a new name written on it? Well, I don't know what the name is, and I don't know for sure what the white stone is, but it could be marble.

Marble is a beautiful stone that people have used for buildings and statues for thousands of years. It is very strong but can still be carved. Even names can be carved into it. Does that remind you of today's verse?

Amazingly, marble is made up of the tiny skeletons and shells of little sea creatures. Over thousands of years, with much heat and pressure, these shells have hardened into marble.

Sometimes things happen in life that hurt us. But just as Jesus causes the broken shells of sea creatures to be turned into something as strong and beautiful as marble, He can cause the things that hurt you to make you stronger and more beautiful for Him. Let Him do His work in you—you'll come out shining when He's done.

Subject of the King

At once I was in the Spirit, and there before me was a throne in heaven with someone sitting on it. And the one who sat there had the appearance of jasper and carnelian. A rainbow, resembling an emerald, encircled the throne. Revelation 4:2, 3.

Heaven. Someday you and I can be there, but today we'll just have to take an imaginary hike to heaven. Our verse tells us there is a throne in heaven. Of course, the "One" sitting on that throne is God. Would you be nervous to see the King of the universe sitting on His throne? It says that the One sitting on the throne looked like jasper and carnelian. We've already discovered that jasper is a type of rock, but do you know what carnelian is? It's a clear, orange-red stone. That must be beautiful!

Why would John, who wrote the book of Revelation, say God looked orange-red and clear? Maybe He meant that God was glowing like fire. I think John was trying to say God's presence fills heaven with light and glory. What a wonderful and glorious God we have. He rules the universe, and He can rule your heart, too. Why don't you ask the King to rule your heart today? Tell Him you'll be His loyal subject.

Signs in the Sky

18 DECEMBER

I watched as he opened the sixth seal. There was a great earthquake. The sun turned black like sackcloth made of goat hair, the whole moon turned blood red. Revelation 6:12.

I love taking night hikes far away from the lights of the city. One of the night-lights I love to look at most is the moon. If you look at the moon through a telescope, you'll see craters and mountains and valleys.

Most of the time you see the moon, it's shining a very bright white. But I've sometimes seen it a scary orange color when it's low in the sky. This happens when the moon's light shines through the dirt and dust floating in the air. Can you imagine how scary the moon would look if it turned a blood-red color? That's what John said would happen not too long before Jesus comes again.

When you read the Bible you find that God gives His people many signs that point to His coming. Are you looking for the signs? Are you reading God's Word to see what they are? Look for the signs of His coming and give Jesus the "I love You" sign when you see Him coming through the clouds.

Just in the Nick of Time

The sky receded like a scroll, rolling up, and every mountain and island was removed from its place. Revelation 6:14.

If you were hiking on an island on the day this verse talks about, you would be in serious trouble. Imagine yourself hiking along and all of a sudden your island disappears into the water below. Can you say, "Swimmin' in your hiking boots"?

There are islands that have appeared and disappeared in the ocean before. They're volcanic islands. Sometimes volcanoes under the ocean erupt and pile up lava until an island is formed. The island of Hawaii is the largest pile of volcanic lava and ashes in the world. There have also been times some small volcanic islands have sunk and disappeared into the ocean. I'm glad I wasn't on that island when it sank!

Our verse today is talking about the day Jesus comes again. Mountains and islands will be falling down and disappearing. Those of us who are His friends have nothing to worry about, though. In fact, we won't even be on the ground when it's all happening. We'll be floating above the disappearing islands into the air to meet Jesus in the clouds. We'll have taken off just in the nick of time.

No More Stinging

They had tails and stings like scorpions, and in their tails they had power to torment people for five months. Revelation 9:10.

Make sure you're wearing your hiking boots today. You see, hiking boots aren't just to keep your feet from hurting when you step on rocks. They can also keep you from getting bit by scorpions.

Have you ever seen a scorpion? They are scary-looking. They have mean-looking pincers and a curved tail with a hollow needle on the end. When they stick that hollow needle-tail into an animal, they pump in poison. Ouch!

Our verse today is talking about people who made war against other nations long ago. Sadly, Satan has caused people since the beginning of time to fight and kill each other.

There are people on the earth today who are making wars and hurting people. You and I may not be able to stop these wars, but we can pray for the people who are hurting—and those who are hurting others. We can pray that God will soften their hearts so they will see the pain they are causing. When we see these wars happening we know that Jesus is coming very soon. Pray for that day when Jesus comes again and the sting of war will happen no more.

Let God Be Your Sunscreen

21 DECEMBER

The fourth angel poured out his bowl on the sun, and the sun was given power to scorch people with fire. Revelation 16:8.

Have you ever been sunburned while hiking? I sure have. My face, my head, my arms, and legs were all red and hurt terribly. Do you know why your skin turns red when you're out in the sun? Some of the sun's rays, called ultraviolet rays, actually damage the surface of your skin, and the tiny blood vessels below the surface break. That sounds pretty bad, doesn't it?

Today's verse tells us about the worst sunburn there will ever be. The book of Revelation talks about plagues and terrible disasters that will come to the earth before Jesus comes again. But don't worry. God will protect His people. He won't let any harm come to those who trust in Him.

You and I should learn to trust in Jesus right now, shouldn't we? We ought to ask Him to lead and guide us each day. As we let God have control of our lives we learn to trust Him more. He's the only one who can save us from the plagues, and He's the only one who can save us from sin. Trust in God today and let Him be your sunscreen.

Come In Out of the Hail

From the sky huge hailstones of about a hundred pounds each fell upon men. And they cursed God on account of the plague of hail, because the plague was so terrible. Revelation 16:21.

When I go hiking in the mountains I have to be prepared. What can start out as a beautiful sunny day may end up in thunder, lightning, and hail. I have been caught in hailstorms in the mountains many times, but the worst hailstorm I've been in was in my own backyard.

Hail is formed when water in clouds freezes into little balls. Those little ice balls get bounced around inside the cloud until they're so heavy they fall to the earth. On this particular summer day the hailstones that fell on me were the size of baseballs. They must have weighed at least one pound. I had to put a bucket over my head to keep from being hit. Windows were smashed, cars were wrecked, and houses had holes in them.

Today's verse talks about hundred-pound hailstones. They will fall to the earth just before Jesus comes again. That will be a frightening day, but if you and I know Jesus we have nothing to worry about. Get to know Him today and come in out of the hail.

Grit Into Grace

*Cargoes of gold, silver, precious stones and pearls;
fine linen, purple, silk and scarlet cloth; every sort
of citron wood, and articles of every kind made of ivory,
costly wood, bronze, iron and marble. Revelation 18:12.*

On today's hike through Revelation we're going to learn about pearls. Perfect, natural pearls are very valuable. They're round and shiny and beautiful. The amazing thing about natural pearls is where they come from. They come from the inside of an oyster. An oyster is an animal that lives in the ocean. It is a soft animal that is protected by two shells that close together like lips. Sometimes when the shell's "lips" are open, a piece of sand will drift into the soft inside. To protect itself from being scratched by the sand, the oyster covers the sand with layers of smooth, hard, shiny material. As many layers of this material cover the grain of sand, a pearl is made.

There are times in life that things bother us, just as the grain of sand bothers the soft inside of the oyster. We could complain and whine a lot, or we could ask God to cover our lives with His grace. Let Him cover you today and watch Him turn grit into grace.

Simply Stunning

The foundations of the city walls were decorated with every kind of precious stone. The first foundation was jasper, the second sapphire, the third chalcedony, the fourth emerald. Revelation 21:19.

This is amazing! Today we're hiking around the walls of the New Jerusalem. They're huge! And they're so stunning. Look at all the stones in the foundation of the wall. There are all kinds of them. Wow, look at that one! It's a beautiful, almost see-through kind of quartz rock called chalcedony.

If you were to take a hike through some of the petrified forests of the western United States, you would find chalcedony in the perfect size and shape of trees. Those trees may have died in Noah's flood. As the tree began to rot, chalcedony and other minerals that settled into the tree at the Flood began to harden. After many years the wood was completely rotted away, and all that was left was chalcedony. If you ever visit Petrified Forest National Park in Arizona, look for the chalcedony trees.

Something that's even more amazing than trees turning to stone is Jesus' turning our sinful stone hearts into hearts of love. It's more amazing than the New Jerusalem walls and chalcedony trees. What Jesus can do with a person's heart is simply stunning.

Glittering in the Dirt

The foundations of the city walls were decorated with every kind of precious stone. The first foundation was jasper, the second sapphire, the third chalcedony, the fourth emerald. Revelation 21:19.

Well, lookie here! We're back hiking in the same verse we were yesterday. We were talking about chalcedony then. Since it's Christmas today, I thought we should talk about a beautiful green gemstone called the emerald. Emeralds are so beautiful, they've been put into the crowns of kings and queens for thousands of years. It's just amazing that a stone so beautiful is found beneath the dirt of the earth.

This is the day we celebrate the birth of the baby Jesus on our earth. Like an emerald, Jesus was a precious gift hidden on our dirty earth. He was born in a barn and grew up in a wicked city. After living among us for 33 years Jesus died on a dirty cross. But even though Jesus was treated like dirt, He really was a gem who showed us what God's love is all about. He showed us that God's love will never give up on us, no matter how dirty we are.

I'm so glad that God's heavenly Gem died for us. Because He did, one day you and I will shine like emeralds in His Holy City in heaven.

Side by Side

The fifth sardonyx, the sixth carnelian, the seventh chrysolite, the eighth beryl, the ninth topaz, the tenth chrysoprase, the eleventh jacinth, and the twelfth amethyst. Revelation 21:20.

Can you believe it? The walls of the New Jerusalem are so huge we're hiking around them for the third day in a row. Today the beautiful stone we're looking at is sardonyx. Sardonyx is very beautiful and made of many layers.

Think of it this way. Pretend you had a red blanket and a white blanket and a brown blanket and a black blanket and you stacked one on top of the other. Then you did the same thing on top of those blankets with more red, black, brown, and white blankets. That would be a colorful stack of blankets, wouldn't it? Well, sardonyx is like that, only the blankets are layers of stone. Imagine all those colors right next to each other.

Our world is a little like that. We have many different kinds of people. Some are different colors, some are from different countries, some speak different languages, some wear different clothes—so many different people, side by side. We are all brothers and sisters, and God loves every one of us. Ask Him to fill your heart with love today. Ask Him to help you love all His kinds of people.

The fifth sardonyx, the sixth carnelian, the seventh chrysolite, the eighth beryl, the ninth topaz, the tenth chrysoprase, the eleventh jacinth, and the twelfth amethyst. Revelation 21:20.

Today we want to look at the tenth stone in the walls of the New Jerusalem. It's called chrysoprase. Actually, chrysoprase is an apple-green type of chalcedony. I wonder why God put two different kinds of the same stone in New Jerusalem's walls. Do you think He ran out of different kinds of stones? I don't think so. There are many beautiful kinds of stones He could have put in the wall. So why did He use two different kinds of the same stone?

Well, I'm very sorry I don't have the answer, but it did make me think of good friends. How did that happen? you say. I think God puts people in our lives who are very much like us to bless us. These are the friends we can play with and talk to and who can know all about us and still love us. They're a little different from us, like chalcedony and chrysoprase, but are so much alike in many ways. Aren't you glad that our God was thoughtful enough to put friends in our lives who are so much like us? He sure must love us!

28 DECEMBER

God's Ways

The fifth sardonyx, the sixth carnelian, the seventh chrysolite, the eighth beryl, the ninth topaz, the tenth chrysoprase, the eleventh jacinth, and the twelfth amethyst. Revelation 21:20.

Can you believe it? We're hiking around the walls of the New Jerusalem for the fifth day in a row. I guess we shouldn't be surprised. After all, each of the walls of the city is hundreds of miles long. Wow!

Today we're looking at the eleventh stone in the city walls. It's called jacinth. Jacinth also goes by another name—zircon. Much of it is found in the faraway country of India. One of the special things about zircon is the way it grows crystals. Many of the stones we know were once liquid. As they cooled they made special shapes. These shapes are called crystals. The most amazing thing is that zircon always makes the same shapes when it cools. It seems to have its own way of doing things.

God is like that too. God has His own way of doing things. We can find His ways in the Bible. God's ways help us to love one another, to be kind to everyone, and to always tell the truth. Read His Word today and find out God's ways of doing things. It's the best way to live life.

Born Twice

29 DECEMBER

The fifth sardonyx, the sixth carnelian, the seventh chrysolite, the eighth beryl, the ninth topaz, the tenth chrysoprase, the eleventh jacinth, and the twelfth amethyst. Revelation 21:20.

Well, this is it. This is the last day we are going to spend hiking around the city walls. The last two days of this year we are going to spend hiking inside the city walls.

The twelfth stone in the city walls is amethyst. I have some amethyst in my rock collection. Not only is it a beautiful shade of purple, but amethyst is also my birthstone. Did you know you have a birthstone? Ask someone what your birthstone is. Each month of the year has its own.

It's fun to celebrate birthdays and collect birthstones, but the day you were born isn't the most important birth date in your life. The most important birth date in your life is the day you are born again.

Being born again means you accept Jesus as the leader of your life. It means you accept that He died on the cross for your sins. It means that you believe Him when He says you have eternal life. It's nice to have a birthstone to celebrate your birth, but it's much better to have a cross that celebrates being born again.

30 DECEMBER

I'll Meet You There

The angel showed me the river of the water of life, as clear as crystal, flowing from the throne of God and of the Lamb. Revelation 22:1.

Oh, isn't it beautiful! Today we've hiked through the gates of the New Jerusalem and into the city. Look, there's an angel coming our way. The angel is so bright. He wants us to follow him. I wonder where he'll take us. . . .

Look at that! It's God's throne. Let's bow down before Him. He's telling us to get up and look at what the angel is showing us. I've never seen such a beautiful river. It's so clear. You can see every rock and fish and plant. There's no pollution or dirt in the water at all.

Don't you wish rivers and lakes and oceans on earth were that clear? They often have so much dirt that fish are sick and it's not safe to drink the water. But everything in heaven is pure. Don't you want a heart as pure as the river of life? I want to live with Jesus so badly. I want to be pure. I want to know God. Drink deeply of Jesus' words today. You can find them in the Bible. Live for Jesus, and I'll meet you at the river of life in heaven.

Hiking Home

On each side of the river stood the tree of life, bearing twelve crops of fruit, yielding its fruit every month. And the leaves of the tree are for the healing of the nations. . . . "Behold, I am coming soon!" Revelation 22:2-7.

I'm a little sad today. It's our very last day of hiking together through the Bible this year. We've discovered nature in every single book in God's Word. We started in Genesis 1 and we're now in the very last chapter of Revelation.

Do you remember the river of life the angel showed us yesterday? Well, if you'll look on either side of it, you'll see a tree with two trunks. One trunk is on each side of the river. The leaves and branches grow together over the river. The tree of life also has 12 types of fruit!

Today's verse also tells us the leaves of the tree are for the "healing of the nations." I think that means God wants us to heal hatred. God is love, and He wants us to live together in love.

Jesus is coming soon! He wants to take everyone to heaven who will believe in Him. Heal those around you by showing them God's love, and don't forget to keep on hiking through the Bible!